KIDDING AROUND

The National Parks of the Southwest

A YOUNG PERSON'S GUIDE

SARAH LOVETT

ILLUSTRATED BY GLEN STROCK

John Muir Publications
Santa Fe, New Mexico

Very special thanks to the rangers and staff of the National Park Service who shared their time and expertise.

John Muir Publications, P.O. Box 613, Santa Fe, NM 87504

First edition. First printing

Library of Congress Cataloging-in-Publication Data
Lovett, Sarah, 1953-
    Kidding around the national parks of the southwest /
    Sarah Lovett; illustrated by Glen Strock. — 1st ed.
        p.   cm.
    Summary: A guide to the natural history, cultural history and sights of interest in the national parks and monuments of the Southwest.
    ISBN 0-945465-72-6
    1. National parks and reserves—Southwest, New—Guide-books—juvenile literature. 2. Southwest, New—Description and travel—1981- —Guide-books—Juvenile literature. 3. Children—Travel—Southwest, New—Guide-books—Juvenile literature. [1. National parks and reserves—Guides. 2. National monuments—Guides. 3. Southwest, New—Description—Guides.]
    I. Strock, Glen, ill. II. Title.
    E160.L66   1990
    917.904'33—dc20   90-39057
                                                                                                      CIP
                                                                                                       AC

Designer: Joanna Hill
Typeface: Trump Medieval
Typesetter: Copygraphics, Santa Fe, New Mexico
Printer: Guynes Printing Company of New Mexico

Distributed to the book trade by:
W. W. Norton & Company, Inc.
New York, New York

Contents

1. The Wild World of National Parks / 5
2. The Bugs and Bears of Low-Impact Camping / 9
3. When the World Began / 12
   Grand Canyon National Park, Arizona / 15
   Canyonlands National Park, Utah / 20
   Capitol Reef National Park, Utah / 25
   Arches National Park, Utah / 28
   Bryce Canyon National Park, Utah / 30
   Zion National Park, Utah / 31
   Dinosaur National Monument, Colorado/Utah / 33
   Petrified Forest National Park, Arizona / 34

4. Fire Mountains / 38
   Capulin National Monument, New Mexico / 41
   Sunset Crater National Monument, Arizona / 43

5. Beneath the Surface of the Earth / 44
   Carlsbad Caverns National Park, New Mexico / 46
   Timpanogos Cave National Monument, Utah / 52
   Great Basin National Park, Nevada / 54

National parks are popular! Plan your trip early and then call or write ahead. Rangers will answer your questions about weather, backcountry permits, and reservations for campgrounds, mule rides, river runs, and other special activities.

Whenever you visit a national park, you must pay a visitor entry fee. This money is used to maintain and protect the park.

6. First People   /   58
   Chaco Canyon National Historical Park,
      New Mexico   /   62
   Canyon de Chelly National Monument,
      Arizona   /   67
   Mesa Verde National Park, Colorado   /   70
   Bandelier National Monument,
      New Mexico   /   73

7. New Worlds   /   75
   El Morro National Monument,
      New Mexico   /   75
   San Antonio Missions National Historic
      Park, Texas   /   77

8. Westward Ho!   /   79
   Fort Union National Monument,
      New Mexico   /   80
   Fort Davis National Historic Site,
      Texas   /   82
   Pipe Spring National Monument,
      Arizona   /   83
   Hubbell Trading Post National Historic
      Site, Arizona   /   86
   Santa Fe Trail National
      Historic Trail   /   87

9. Dare of the Desert   /   88
   Big Bend National Park, Texas   /   90
   Death Valley National Monument,
      California   /   92
   Joshua Tree National Monument,
      California   /   99
   White Sands National Monument,
      New Mexico   /   102

10. Back to the Future   /   104

Appendix   /   106

1. The Wild World of National Parks

Wilderness is not just forests and mountains. It includes deserts, icebergs and glaciers, oceans, and caves. Maybe we should call it wild-er-ness!

WWWWWWWoooooooowwwwwwwww!!!! Where's the best place to see hundreds of bats air dive into caves at speeds of 25 miles per hour and more? Where can you descend 800 feet below the earth's surface to wander through a geologic garden of stalactites, stalagmites, and stone toadstools? Where's the wildest place to witness a red-hot volcanic eruption?

A national park, of course!

National parks, monuments, and historic sites in the United States cover more than 79 million acres, including rivers, canyons, mountains, caves, volcanoes, forests, deserts, and seashores. That's a lot of territory for you to explore, treasure, and protect for the future. The National Park System represents some of the last wilderness land on our planet!

Hunters and Gatherers, Movers and Shakers

Native Americans, the early inhabitants of what is now America, lived with the land for centuries without disturbing its natural balance. They gathered nuts and berries, hunted only the animals they needed for food, and grew small crops of corn and vegetables. Their lives revolved

around the cycles of nature. They did not have factories, machines, or crowded cities like those people who came later.

The first European immigrants to sail to the New World in the 1600s had little in common with Native Americans. They brought dreams of progress to their new country. There were industries to develop, fortunes to make, and lands to civilize. That land seemed never-ending.

For 300 years, trees were chopped down to build towns and fuel factories. Ground was cleared to plant crops and graze cattle and sheep. Great cities grew up where swamps and forests had been before. The most determined settlers moved slowly westward, forever altering the earth that lay in their paths.

Finally, by the late 1800s, many people were tired of living in overcrowded and polluted cities. They had witnessed the exploitation of natural resources in the race for money, material goods, and the trappings of prosperity.

In 1901, Teddy Roosevelt became the nation's first environmentalist president. While serving in the White House, he approved 5 new national parks and created 53 wildlife reserves and 16 national monuments (including the very first, Devil's Tower National Monument in Wyoming).

Just like today, those people began to fear they were losing something irreplaceable and crucial to life—clean air, pure water, green forests, diverse plants, wild animals, unique insects, and open space. They decided to set aside and conserve special wilderness areas. They named these very special places national parks.

The first national park was created in 1872 when the United States Congress reserved the awesome mountains and valleys of Yellowstone as "a public park or pleasuring-ground for the benefit and enjoyment of the people."

On August 25, 1916, the National Park Service became the official caretaker of our national parks. Park rangers are the people who live and work in parks, monuments, and historic sites. Part of their job is to keep humans from upsetting the balance of nature. But rangers can only do so much; it's up to us to do the rest. Today, there are many people and organizations dedicated to the protection and preservation of unspoiled wilderness.

*Who are those people with the Smokey Bear brown hats? Uniforms make **rangers** easy to spot when you need to know about shield volcanoes, Mexican free-tail bats, or which trails are open to wheelchairs. They also enforce the rules. Always obey park regulations! They exist to protect you in the park and to protect the park from you. Even with the best intentions, human beings can seriously upset the balance of nature.*

2. The Bugs and Bears of Low-Impact Camping

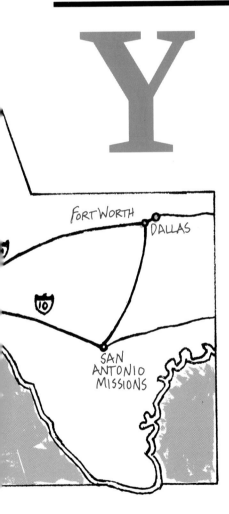

Your mission is to have a great wilderness adventure and yet leave no trace of your visit behind you. The first thing to do (if you're not going to stay in a regular park campground) is get a special backcountry permit from a park ranger. Rangers have safety information to give you *before* you start—things like fire danger, weather warnings, and special regulations.

Another important purpose of backcountry permits is to let the rangers know where you are—and where to look for you in case of emergencies. *Always* take an adult on your adventure. *Always* tell your family and friends where you're going and when you'll return.

After You? No, After You . . .

What do you do when you meet a panther, deer, or rattlesnake along the trail? Don't forget *they* live here, you're just visiting. Your job is to disturb as little as possible and that includes four-legged beasts and slithery reptiles.

When you arrive at a park, ask a ranger about local wildlife you're likely to meet. Rangers will give you important tips on the best way to handle wildlife encounters.

Thirsty?

Carry drinking water, and don't forget to drink it! More than one camper has become dehydrated (de-watered) with a half-full canteen. Make it a habit to quench your thirst regularly.

Are you in country where there are rivers, streams, springs, or potholes? Most water is contaminated with minerals, bacteria, and parasites that can make you very sick! You must boil water for at least one full minute before drinking.

Do not put your soapy dishes or your soapy body directly into a water supply. Don't forget, one of the nice things about backcountry camping is getting dirty and staying dirty!

The Well-Dressed Camper

Hikers should always be well dressed. That doesn't mean you need designer labels on your clothes. Comfort is what counts. And be prepared for a change in the weather. Bring: a compass, a flashlight, a full canteen, power-packed food, sunscreen, sunglasses, sturdy shoes, extra warm clothes, and a small first-aid kit. Insect repellent is a good idea even though it doesn't always make the bugs buzz off. If you need special medication, don't forget to include it!

Setting Up Camp

Choose a campsite because it's good for the environment, not because it's good for you. That means at least ½ mile (and out of sight and sound) from park roads, trails, and developed areas. Your site should be located at least 100 yards from a water source.

No campfires! Use liquid- or gas-fueled camp

stoves only for cooking and heating water. (Make sure an adult supervises any camp stove action!)

Bury human waste at least six inches deep and at least a hundred yards from water sources, trails, and campsites. Other waste (or trash) needs to be carried out with you.

With a bit of practice you can become a veteran hiker, camper, and wilderness explorer. But remember, nature is always the teacher and you are always the student—no matter how old you are.

3. When the World Began

The grind! Erosion happens in different angles. Fine-grained, hard sandstones and limestones erode into sharp vertical cliffs and ledges. Shale and mudstone grind away into softer slopes and hills. See if you can pick out what's what!

uppose there was a recipe for making Planet Earth. To begin with, you'd need lots of 5-billion-year-old whizzing meteors and whirling gases that swirl together and harden into a globe. And, of course, you must stir the globe at the perfect speed around the sun and keep the temperature just so. You should also add gravity to pull iron and nickel, the heaviest elements, to the core. Then glop almost 2,000 miles of bubbling, hot rock on top. That would give you a basic earth "pie," but what about all the incredible mountains, valleys, oceans, and deserts topping earth? What about the crust?

Geology is the study of the earth, its formation, and the development of its layers. National parks are heaven for geologists. At the Grand Canyon, you can stand at the edge of a cliff and peer down a mile, all the way to the Precambrian era that ended about 600 million years ago. Surprisingly, that's just a wink in earth years.

Oh, Grow Up!
Mountains don't grow on trees. They form in a variety of ways. Some are carved by great **glaciers**

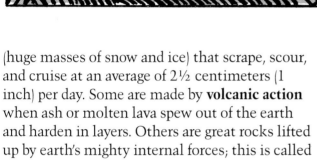

(huge masses of snow and ice) that scrape, scour, and cruise at an average of 2½ centimeters (1 inch) per day. Some are made by **volcanic action** when ash or molten lava spew out of the earth and harden in layers. Others are great rocks lifted up by earth's mighty internal forces; this is called **thrusting and faulting**.

What Grows Up, Must Grow Down

The land around you is constantly changing. Nothing is forever, not even mountains. Sure, a mountain is a mountain for a very long time, but wind, water, and gravity are always at work wearing it down. This wearing down is called **erosion**. Besides wind and water, ice and ocean waves are also good at wearing down rock. When rocks are exposed to any of the "big five," they **weather**. That means they weaken and crumble into tiny bits of sand and dirt that easily blow and wash away. When enough bits land on dry ground and pile up, or land in water and sink to the bottom, they're called **sediment**.

Many national parks in the desert Southwest are related when it comes to geology. What you learn about rocks in one park will often help you understand their "rock relatives" in other parks.

Rock and Roll

Have you ever wanted to name a rock? Well, there are three basic types of rock on earth. **Igneous** rock forms from molten material deep inside the earth. It's hot, fiery liquid that hardens when it cools off. **Sedimentary** rock comes in bits and pieces. Tiny grains of rock, shells, and minerals settle down together to form a layer of rock (like a cake with lots of different colored layers). **Sandstone**, **shale**, **limestone**, and **conglomerates** found in the Canyon Country of Utah are all examples of sedimentary rock. **Metamorphic** rock begins as igneous or sedimentary rock and then is baked in a giant pressure cooker, the earth. The **Vishnu Schist** layer at the base of the Grand Canyon is one example of metamorphic rock.

Make Your Own Sediment

If you've always wanted to create sediment, here's your chance. You'll need a glass quart jar and lid, small stones, sand and dirt (½ cup each), and 2 cups of water. Put everything into the jar and tighten the lid. Shake, shake, shake it up. Place the jar on a flat counter or shelf and wait. Watch as gravel, sand, and soil slowly settle on the bottom. Which settles out first? (The heavy gravels, of course.) Now imagine each layer has hardened into rock like the layers you'll see at the Grand Canyon, Bryce, or Dinosaur national parks.

GRAND CANYON NATIONAL PARK, ARIZONA

Grand Canyon National Park has been called the biggest, the mostest, the oldest, the bestest, the

KAIBAB LODGE
DEL MONTE
NORTH RIM ENTRANCE
PORT IMPERIAL
BRIGHT ANGEL
NORTH RIM
CAPE ROYAL

longest, and the veryest. You might call it awesome, or your mouth might drop silently open. Either way, a view of the Grand Canyon, and the millions of earth years it represents, will boggle your mind.

The park is filled with things to do—hiking, trail rides, river rides, and ranger programs. You'll see petroglyphs, mule deer, potsherds, and prehistoric fossils.

The Grand Canyon is actually three different parks in one: the **South Rim**, the **North Rim**, and the **Inner Canyon** where you can river raft down the Colorado River. The North Rim (open mid-May to October only) is great to visit because there are less people and there is more nature. Hikes all the way down to the Inner Canyon are hard work. Most people visit the South Rim because it's open year-round and you don't have to hike to get there.

South Rim
Grand Canyon Village, on the South Rim, is a city in itself with a post office, a bank, a gas station, an amphitheater, a school, hotels, museums, a grocery store, and even a jail.

The **Visitor Center** is your starting point. To learn about the natural and human history of the park, there's a 15-minute slide show, a bookstore, and park rangers on duty to answer questions. If you're a river raft buff, check out the great exhibits. This is also where you can find out about ranger programs such as guided nature walks and special activities.

Nearby, the **Rim Trail** is a fairly flat 14-kilometer (9-mile) stretch along the canyon rim from Hermits Rest to Mather Point. The trail is paved between Maricopa Point and Yavapai

Point. You might stroll over to the **Yavapai Geologic Museum** where exhibits show you how the canyon came to be. Don't miss the chance to view every type of boat that has journeyed the treacherous Colorado River. Try to imagine how the trip would feel in a canoe or a log raft.

Three Left Feet

Most people drive to the Grand Canyon. And then they drive around the Grand Canyon. Or they take a tour bus. Some lucky ducks float by boat along the Colorado River. And some saddlejacks "sit in" the canyon by pack mule. But what about your own two feet? Hiking at the Grand Canyon is an incredible way to see nature in action. It's also challenging, even to the most experienced hikers. Following park rules might save your life. Always hike with a grown-up. Check with a park ranger before you start. Stay on marked trails. Carry plenty of drinking water and food. Wear sturdy shoes or hiking boots and proper clothes. And don't forget that after you hike down, you must hike back up!

Desert View is a 15-minute stroll 26 miles east of Grand Canyon Village. It offers amazing views.

On **Tusayan Ruin Walk**, it takes you only 20 minutes to step back 800 years in history. These are the ruins of ancient homes that early canyon dwellers made.

Bright Angel Trail begins near Bright Angel Lodge. It's a 2½-mile round-trip hike to the resthouse, and water is available from May through September. If you continue to **Indian Garden** (about 6 hours round-trip), you can picnic in this pretty and shady oasis.

One-third; two-thirds. Treks into the canyon always start downhill and end uphill. To pace yourself, decide how long you want to hike. When you've walked one-third of that time, turn around and start back. It takes twice as long to go uphill as down.

*Who goes there? Who went here? The **Tusayan Museum** near Desert View on the South Rim is the place to find out about prehistoric and modern inhabitants of the area. Explore exhibits, ask questions, and then guide yourself through ancient Pueblo Indian ruins.*

Four-legged trips by mule into the canyon are fun and very popular. Some dates are reserved a whole year in advance! No last-minute mules, that's for sure. Also, you must be over 12 years old to "drive" a mule.

Would you want to explore hundreds of miles of wild, uncharted river in a small, wooden boat? That's what John Wesley Powell, the famous geologist and one-armed Civil War veteran, did in 1869 and again in 1871. Many of his theories about the geology of the canyon are still considered valid after more than 100 years.

Fossils, Fossils Everywhere

If you're feeling like a fossil (finding one, that is), ask a ranger about the **West Rim Worship Site** on the South Rim. It's on the Rim Trail, near Bright Angel Lodge, past the mule corral and about 200 yards beyond the West Rim Interchange. Keep your eyes peeled. Do you spy sponges, brachiopods, or coral?

Perhaps you'd like some fossils "to go," but you know you can't take souvenirs. Well, you'll need a crayon or pencil, a piece of clean white paper, and very gentle hands. When you find your fossil, place the paper carefully on top and lightly rub back and forth with the crayon or pencil. Your "fossil rubbing" should appear like magic with a little elbow grease.

Take Time . . .

At Grand Canyon National Park, take the time to ask a ranger a question . . . and another question . . . and another question!

CANYONLANDS NATIONAL PARK, UTAH

Four different parks in one—that's Canyonlands National Park. Canyonlands has something for everyone. If you want a view that's worthy of standing on clouds, try **Island in the Sky**. A tangle of remote canyons and wilderness for you? **The Maze**, of course. Rocky spires and pinnacles, archaeological ruins, and open country may all be found in **The Needles**. And then there's **The Rivers**. If you crave rapid adventure with twenty-foot waves and foam on top, or nice and easy cruising, the Green and Colorado rivers shake hands in Canyonlands National Park, and you're invited along for the ride. All you need do in

Endangered! *Peregrine falcons and bald eagles are two endangered species who find a safe haven in Canyonlands National Park. Wilderness areas provide habitats for many birds and animals who can't survive elsewhere.*

return is treat this awesome wilderness with the respect and care it deserves!

Island in the Sky

First stop is the **Visitor Center**. Park rangers will answer your questions. You'll also have the chance to pick up books, brochures, weather reports, a schedule of park programs, and back-country camping permits.

As you drive along Island Road, there are many self-guided trails to hike. For instance, **Neck Spring Trail** begins 0.4 mile south of the Visitor Center and loops for 5 miles. Plan on 3 or 4 hours of exercise, and carry water.

Look for water troughs, old hitching posts, and other cowboy paraphernalia because Neck Spring was a watering hole for livestock in the old days. Some cowboys used tin cans around the legs of tables to keep the mice from joining dinner.

You might also spot hummingbirds, squirrels, chipmunks, mule deer, and bighorn sheep near the trail. If you notice white, orange, or brown rock chippings in the sand, these could be the remains of ancient Anasazi toolmaking efforts. Remember, leave them where you find them so others can discover them in the future.

Another hike, **Mesa Arch Trail**, loops you through a piñon and juniper woodland. Can you tell the blackbrush from the juniper? The yucca from the prickly pear cactus? Has it been raining or snowing here lately? One way to find out is to check the round pads of the prickly pear. Plump means recent moisture; not so plump means dry. The prickly pear stores water for thirsty times.

When you reach the edge of the mesa, there's

Wolf, wolf! There used to be wolves in much of the Southwest but not anymore. Loss of habitat and attempts by humans to destroy wolves have driven them away from their natural homes. The National Park Service wants to restore the gray wolf to Yellowstone and Glacier national parks. But that will only happen after we humans understand and appreciate the wolf as a natural (and fascinating) member of the ecosystem and not a fairy-tale "bad guy"!

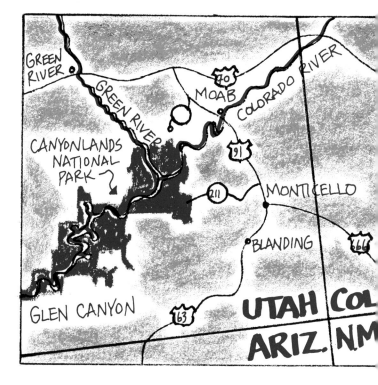

Mesa Arch with the **La Sal Mountains** peeking through. Did you guess those mountains are about 35 miles away? Two thousand feet below you, the Colorado River Gorge winds its way along. Since you're already looking down, see the woman leaning over her washtub? Actually, it's an arch named **Washer Woman**.

If you camp at **Willow Flat Campground**, you're only a few miles from **Upheaval Dome**. What caused this dome to form? Was it an ancient meteor that crashed into earth? Bbbbbooooommmmmmmmm!!! Or was it layers of salt deep underground which pushed up the rock above? Take the 25-minute trail and decide for yourself.

*"Get your big feet off me!" Superman had nothing to do with the desert's **cryptogamic soil**. This black, crusty stuff below your feet is alive with algae, fungi, mosses, lichens, and bacteria. This living soil prevents erosion and retains water so bigger plants can take root. Cryptogamic soil is a tiny plant community working together. No, don't step on it, it's fragile and it's alive!*

The Maze

It's a jungle out there! Actually, it's a desert and a wild, wild world. This section of the park is known for its wilderness. Don't forget, nature is the boss.

The Maze is a sandstone labyrinth that is about 30 miles square and very confusing. For centuries, people avoided the rugged tangle of cliffs and canyons, but after ranching developed in the area, cowboys had to search for water and stray livestock.

It only takes bumping over 40 miles of 4-wheel-drive roads to reach the **Doll House** in the Maze District. Once there you're surrounded by a fairyland of colorful castles, towers, giants,

*Horseshoe Canyon (a separate strip of park west of the Green River) is famous for the **Great Gallery** where prehistoric rock art figures larger than you date back two or three thousand years.*

Pothole Point is the place to examine some very small creatures. Potholes are formed by erosion, and when it rains or snows they fill with water. Bats, birds, deer, and all the locals drink here. But look closer and see who lives here.

Ant traps? As you hike the *Cave Spring Loop*, look out for ant lions. These tiny insect larvae build teensy pits in the sand below cliff over-hangs. These traps catch...ants, what else!

and pinnacles—some as high as a 10-story building —made of sandstone. Climb around and explore. Walk to the cliff edge and wave at the tiny Colorado River far below you. If it's hot, you'll find shade. If it's windy, stop, look, and listen to it howl!

Remember, wherever you go, The Maze is wilderness; leave no trace of your visit behind you.

The Needles

The Needles District has its own Visitor Center because there are so many things to do here. Ask a ranger to help you choose what's right for you.

Hiking? **Cave Spring Loop Trail** leads you over slickrock and two ladders to reach Cave Spring and the old cowboy line camp. There's an easy shortcut if you reverse your route.

Roadside Ruin Loop Trail is a short walk to an ancient Indian granary used to store corn, nuts, and seeds.

The Needles is great for camping, petroglyphs, or wilderness adventure, too. Just like The Maze, there is backcountry to visit. A 4-wheel drive over **Elephant Hill** means start and stop, back up and bump all the way. Maybe it should be called "back and forth" country.

At Elephant Hill, a jeep trail leads to just short of the canyon rim. Look down and see the con-fluence (meeting) of the Colorado and Green rivers. Are they different colors? A red river means red dirt washing downstream.

Another trail leads to **The Needles** them-selves, tall red and white rock skyscrapers. If you continue from here, you'll reach the **Joint Trail**, a big crack in the rocks that takes you to **Chesler Park**, a green and lovely oasis.

The Rivers

Explorer John Wesley Powell rode the wild rapids of the Colorado River through what was to become Canyonlands in 1869. Below the confluence of the Green and Colorado rivers, 23 kilometers (14 miles) of wild and wooly rapids roar through **Cataract Canyon**. In spring, waves may reach heights of 20 feet. River trips are popular and guaranteed to thrill you. Guided raft trips should be arranged privately in nearby towns. Ask park rangers for information.

Take Time . . .

At Canyonlands National Park, take the time to sit on an ancient rock and watch the sun set.

CAPITOL REEF NATIONAL PARK, UTAH

A yellow-bellied marmot. The Waterpocket Fold. A spadefoot toad. Fruit picking. Cathedral Valley. Indian paintbrush. These are a few of the life forms, places, activities, and geological formations that await you at Capitol Reef National Park.

Capitol Reef is a long, narrow park that follows the Waterpocket Fold. The **Visitor Center** is roughly in the middle of the park. So are the **Old Fruita Schoolhouse**, the **Fruita Orchards**, the **petroglyphs**, the **campground**, and **Fremont River Trail** where you might get whistled at by yellow-bellied marmots.

Hickman Bridge Trail is two miles from the Visitor Center. The hike includes a gentle climb to Hickman Natural Bridge, which is a 133-foot-wide sandstone bridge. On the way, you'll pass a "pit house" foundation and a granary used by the

*A **waterpocket fold** is not part of your raincoat. It's a geologic formation something like a giant 100-mile wrinkle. About 65 million years ago, in what is now south central Utah and Capitol Reef National Park, pressures deep in the earth heaved and buckled and pushed up into a giant fold of rock.*

Fremont people. Take the time to close your eyes and imagine what life was like here so long, long ago.

Chimney Rock Canyon Trail is a full-day 9-mile jaunt for the hardy. Bring water, wear a hat, and wear "wet" shoes because you get to wade the river at the crossing. Ask the ranger for a weather report before you begin.

Petroglyph Pullout just a mile from the Visitor Center is the place to see some wonderful rock art. Binoculars are handy here. Follow the path at the base of the cliff. Can you spot many hard-to-see figures, faces, and masks? What do they mean? Your guess may be as good as the experts'; what's your theory?

Where Are the People?

The **Fremont River** flows through the Capitol Reef country of the Waterpocket Fold. Fremont peoples moved near the river as early as A.D. 700. These ancient Native Americans were neighbors of another ancient culture to the south, the Anasazi. Later, Ute and Paiute Indians hunted along the river and roamed the area.

What's in a name?
Fremont River is named for explorer John Charles Frémont who lived in the 19th century. Later, the Fremont Indians were named after the river even though they lived here more than a thousand years ago.

In the late 1800s, **Mormon pioneers** began to settle in Fremont Valley, and by the next century, they were producing delicious fruit from their orchards. After Capitol Reef became a national monument (and later a national park), the Mormans moved away. Today, you can still visit the Old Fruita Schoolhouse where children learned their ABCs, and you may even pick fresh fruit in season.

Take Time...
On your visit to Capitol Reef National Park, take the time to slow down and think about how long the earth has been spinning around in space. The rocks surrounding you tell the story if you listen carefully.

Fruita Orchards (more than 2,500 trees) are irrigated with the same ditch system that the Mormon pioneers used. Fremont Indians used a similar method 700 years earlier. If it's fruit season, ask about cherry, apricot, peach, pear, and apple picking.

*In 1890, 12-year-old Nettie Behunin was teaching school! The **Fruita One-Room Schoolhouse** wasn't built until 1896. Nettie was still teaching then, and if you do your arithmetic you'll know how old she was that year.*

Civil War veteran John Wesley Wolfe settled here in 1888. You can visit the rustic log cabin, root cellar, and corral that he and his son, Fred, built. **Wolfe Ranch** *is a flash of the past.*

ARCHES NATIONAL PARK, UTAH

Where will you find the greatest density of arches in the world? Arches National Park, that's where! Uplift, erosion, and millions of years are responsible for this wonderland of rocks.

Stop at the **Visitor Center** and orient yourself. There's a slide show, a geology museum, and history exhibits. During summer months, ask about special programs and about **Fiery Furnace Walk** when a naturalist leads the way. **Devil's Garden Campground** has spaces available on a first-come basis. Arrive early!

Feet Feats

Stroll along **Devil's Garden Trail** (3.2 kilometers/ 2 miles) from the trailhead to **Double O Arch**. There's also a new primitive loop trail for the able-bodied.

In the Windows section of the park, easy walks of less than an hour take you to four major arches: North and South Windows, Turret Arch, and Double Arch.

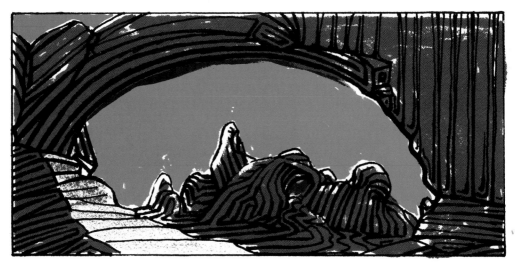

High on Highlights

Park Avenue looks like a New York skyline with its spires and fins. **Balanced Rock** makes you catch your breath as you gaze at this world-famous balancing act. **Panorama Point** offers a view of Salt Valley and the Fiery Furnace. This is best at sunset. **Skyline Arch** is twice as big as it was before 1940 when a boulder fell out. **Delicate Arch** is a rainbow of colors. Depending on the time of day and year, you'll see pink, gold, red, blue, yellow, or green. It's as tall as a four-story building and perched on the edge of a cliff. When winter water freezes in the cracks of this arch, the ice takes more space than water. Cracks become larger and pieces fall away. Some day, Delicate Arch will collapse, and new arches will continue to form.

North Window and **South Window** are matching holes; from the far side, they look like a pair of eyeglasses, and then they're called **The Spectacles**.

Landscape Arch, a one-mile stroll on the Devil's Garden Trail, is one of the longest known natural stone arches in the world—306 feet long!

Take Time...

Local fauna at Arches National Park includes the midget faded rattlesnake, the desert cottontail, the foot-long collared lizard, and the red-tailed hawk. Mule deer are often seen early in the morning or at sunset near campgrounds. On your visit, take time to learn more about one of these wonderful creatures.

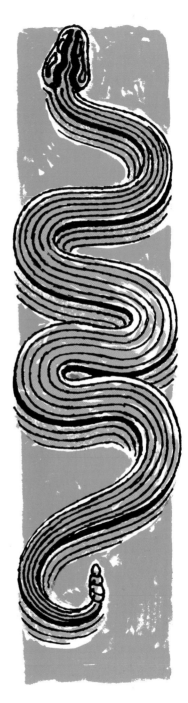

BRYCE CANYON NATIONAL PARK, UTAH

An amazing maze of rocky spires, pinnacles, and monuments, Bryce Canyon National Park might appear like a gigantic "rock garden." Besides boasting incredible geologic formations, the park also serves as a refuge for endangered peregrine falcons and threatened Utah prairie dogs. Mountain lions live here. So do the gray fox and the white-breasted nuthatch. And you can, too, for a day or a week.

Begin at the **Visitor Center** to learn about the history and geology of the park as well as special program schedules. During summer months, there are programs for kids and grown-ups. Ranger-guided natural history walks and talks are terrific. And there's even a **Jr. Ranger Program**!

Hoodoos You Think They Are?

The **Hoodoos** are very famous. So who are the hoodoos? Rock pinnacles or pillars, shaped by erosion. When you gaze at miles of hoodoos in the park, what do you see? A science fiction city? Marching rock-people? Millions of years of the earth's geologic history?

Giddy-up!

Guided horseback trail rides are a terrific way to explore the park. Morning and afternoon excursions begin at the corral near Bryce Canyon Lodge. Rides are only available during the summer, spring, and fall, and reservations should be made in advance.

Snowshoes and Skis

Winter is a great time to visit Bryce. Ski cross-country on **Fairyland Ski Trail** and **Paria Ski**

Trail. If you don't ski, don't worry! Snowshoes are available at the Visitor Center. They are loaned free of charge if someone in your group has a valid driver's license. Ask rangers for details.

Take Time . . .

While visiting Bryce Canyon National Park, take time to "adopt a trail." Carry a bag on your hike, and collect litter as you walk. Other visitors and park residents will greatly appreciate your efforts!

ZION NATIONAL PARK, UTAH

Not only is Zion National Park famous for geology, it's also home to unique plants, animals, fungi, insects, bacteria, and other living things. Their park is yours to share as long as you treat it with respect. Choose from hiking, biking, horseback riding, wading, and camping. Picnic at the **Grotto Picnic Area**, cool off carefully in the **Virgin River**, join the **Jr. Ranger Program** in summer months, and always remember to ask rangers lots of questions about biodiversity, ecosystems, and other important subjects.

   Zion Canyon Visitor Center (at the south entrance) is your introduction to the park. With a museum, a slide show, books, videos, maps, and permits, there's plenty to see and do. **Kolob Canyons Visitor Center** also has information, books, backcountry permits, and rangers. Weather and safety tips and schedules of special park events are available at both centers. Spring through fall, ask about guided trail rides at **Zion Lodge.**

Cycles! *Bicycling is a wonderful way to cruise Zion National Park from November to March. That's when car traffic is lightest. For your own safety, rules are important! No riding on trails or cross-country. Main roads are open to bicycles, but traffic can be heavy. Early a.m. and late afternoon are good times for you. Wear a helmet and bright clothes, carry water, and always travel with a grown-up. A vehicle must carry your bike through* **Zion-Mt. Carmel Tunnel**.

High on a Hike!

You call yourself a hiker? Zion offers many trails to wear out your sneakers or hiking boots. **Weeping Rock** (0.2 mile) is paved, shady, and easy going for nature buffs. **Canyon Overlook** (1 mile) is a little more difficult, but the awesome view of lower **Zion Canyon** is worth the huff and puff. If you're in the mood for an easy stroll along the Virgin River, **Gateway to the Narrows** (2 miles) is the ticket. Baby strollers and wheelchairs are invited, too. Keep your eyes open for animal tracks along the trails.

Want to hear the rumble of a waterfall? The trail to **Emerald Pools** will take you there (1 mile, strollers and wheelchairs OK). If you continue to the upper pool, plan on 2.2 miles round-trip.

Other trails to **Watchman**, **Hidden Canyon**, **Angels Landing**, and **Taylor Creek** are more strenuous. Ask a ranger for details.

Take Time . . .

While you're visiting Zion National Park, take the time to lie down on your tummy and view the teeny, tiny residents who live and work down here.

DINOSAUR NATIONAL MONUMENT, COLORADO/UTAH

Stegosaurus, Diplodocus, Apatosaurus (humongous), and the much smaller *Camptosaurus* all browsed and grazed here. The fierce, razor-toothed *Allosaurus* hunted here. Where? Dinosaur National Monument, of course.

On your visit, you'll see a great fossil bed (or quarry), filled with dinosaur bones, in the Dinosaur Quarry building. But this monument offers even more than dinosaurs. Prehistoric Fremont people carved petroglyphs (rock art) in the cliffs around A.D. 200–1300. Explorer and scientist John Wesley Powell floated down the Green River in 1869 and 1871, and you can do the same today! In the park's canyon wilderness area, rocks with fossils two and three times older than the dinosaurs have been exposed by uplift and erosion. There's hiking, camping, river rafting, and fishing.

No Bones About It
Monument Headquarters Visitor Center (3 kilometers east of the city of Dinosaur, Colo.) is the official gateway to the wilderness canyon area. Don't look for fossils here. Instead, watch a quick slide show to learn about the park. This is also the place to check out summer ranger programs and ask about backcountry trails and permits.

Harpers Corner Scenic Drive leads you into the monument from the Visitor Center. The two-hour hike at **Harpers Corner** is a terrific way to get your exercise as you view the awesome canyons and rivers below you.

Paleontologist Earl Douglass began to hunt for dinosaur bones in the area that is now Dinosaur National Monument in 1908. Eventually, Douglass dug up thousands of bones, including several almost complete skeletons. Today, scientists uncover (but do not remove) bones from the site at the Dinosaur Quarry building. In summer months, watch Quarry paleontologists at work.

Bighorns! *If you spot bighorn sheep at Dinosaur, please report to a ranger how many, where, when, and who. Both sexes have horns. Adult males (rams) have big horns that curve like a giant "C". Females (ewes) have shorter, spiky horns. The NPS is trying to ensure a healthy bighorn population at the monument.*

Jones Hole is another place to hike—this time along a tree-lined clear spring creek.

Make no bones about it, the **Dinosaur Quarry building** (in the Western corner of the monument) is fossil heaven for professional and amateur paleontologists alike. Dinosaur, turtle, crocodile, and clam fossils are preserved in the sands of an ancient river. Dissolved silica seeped into layers of sediment and the riverbed hardened into sandstone while the bones became mineralized.

Fishing is possible (with proper licensing) in the monument, but many area species of fish are endangered and the river is muddy. The best way to get wet is by **river rafting**. You'll experience the history and geology of the park just as early explorers did, and you'll have a terrific ride, too! Ask rangers about raft trip arrangements.

PETRIFIED FOREST NATIONAL PARK, ARIZONA

Have you ever been petrified, scared stiff, so frightened you're frozen in stone? Well, petrified wood isn't wood that got scared, but it is wood that has hardened into stone. The forests of Petrified Forest National Park date back more than 225 million years to the late Triassic.

In prehistoric times, a great forest grew near the banks of a stream. These trees grew to be 200 to 250 feet tall! Ferns, cycads, and very weird plants covered the surrounding flatlands where crocodile- and salamander-like reptiles and early dinosaurs slithered and lumbered.

Now, millions of years later, you're invited to lumber around those very same trees. They're not standing up but scattered more like giant pickup sticks. Many are located miles from their original roots. How did they travel? Not by bus, that's for sure.

During ancient floods, the trees were washed into the floodplain and covered by mud and volcanic ash. This earth cover kept out oxygen, and the trees were preserved. Slowly, silica-rich groundwater (silica is a mineral that keeps things dry) seeped into the logs and eventually the wood was encased by silica. Over many, many years, tiny quartz crystals formed in wood cells. Some of these crystals became semi-precious gemstones. This is a very, very simple explanation of how this ancient forest petrified.

For millions of years the land sank, flooded, and was lifted up again to sea level. The uplift cracked the logs into chunks. Eventually, wind and water eroded the earth sediments that covered the trees. The colorful logs you see today are just another "phase" in earth's geologic growth chart. In fact, in some areas of the park, hidden fossils and logs are still buried as far as 90 meters (300 feet) below your feet. Some day, water and wind will expose these, too.

Pass Go

Petrified Forest National Park is almost three different parks—the Painted Desert in the north, archaeological sites in the middle, and lots of petrified wood in the south.

Watch a 17-minute film on how wood petrifies at the **Painted Desert Visitor Center** (north end of the park). At **Rainbow Forest Museum** (south end), explore exhibits of neat petrified wood specimens, and learn about the area's geologic history and the ancient peoples who lived here 2,000 years ago. North or south, the visitor cen-

Prehistoric Indians used petrified wood to make arrowheads and tools. They also traded it for shells and other special things. Early Navajo thought the petrified logs were the bones of a humongous monster named Yietso who had been killed by the ancient ancestors of the Navajo.

ter is the place to find out about hiking, wilderness camping permits, maps, and weather conditions.

If you're cruising, there's a 43-kilometer (27-mile) scenic route with eight overlooks along the rim of the **Painted Desert**. At **Kachina Point**, see the **Painted Desert Inn** built in the 1920s and rebuilt by the Civilian Conservation Corps (CCC). In the 1930s, the CCC was established by President Franklin D. Roosevelt to help the nation survive the Great Depression. The Painted Desert Inn is now a National Historic Landmark.

The **Tepees** are "badlands," which means it's a pretty bad place to try to make a living. These rock "tents" are the result of erosion, and their color is courtesy of iron, manganese, and other generous minerals.

Check out **Blue Mesa** for awesome pedestal logs.

The **Crystal Forest** was named for logs whose cracks were filled with shimmering clear quartz

and glittering amethyst crystals. Now the cracks are empty because early gem hunters vandalized the area. The bad part is you can't see those magical gems anymore; the good part is these gem hunters caused people to ask the government to preserve the area as a national monument—and it did!

Hikes

For long hikes, you must check with a ranger first. Several short hikes are fun and easy, but short or long, carry water. **Long Logs/Agate House** is an .08-kilometer (half-mile) loop trail. Follow it to some of the longest logs in the Petrified Forest. You may also take the turn-off (.04 kilometer/one-quarter mile) to Agate House, a seven-room house that dates back to A.D. 1150.

Take Time . . .

While visiting Petrified Forest National Park, take time to look at a petroglyph and think about the early people who lived here.

A dinosaur named "Gertie." Fossils of weird dinosaurs, reptiles, fish, and plants have been found at Petrified Forest National Park. "Gertie" was discovered in 1984. Paleontologists (scientists who study fossils) are puzzled by Gertie and her relationship to other dinosaur family members. Some day Gertie's bones will be displayed at the park.

4. Fire Mountains

Ever blow your top? Spout off? Vent yourself? Get all fired up or really steamed? You're not alone. That's just what active volcanoes like Kilauea and Mauna Loa on Hawaii do. Erupting volcanoes put on a great show, and while they're at it, they also make mountains and increase the size of islands.

In ancient times, people had many explanations for volcanic eruptions. Some said Vulcan, the god of fire, had a hot and steamy workshop underground where he forged great spears and swords of steel. Others believed the earth was angry when she erupted. Hoping to calm things down, they offered sacrificial gifts—food, clothing, jewelry, and even other humans—to the gods they worshiped. Now we have scientific explanations for volcanoes, and we don't have to believe the earth is in a bad mood.

Dead or Alive?

If a volcano erupts all the time, like Kilauea, it's **active**. If it only goes off every once in a while, like Mount Etna in Sicily, call it **intermittent**. Volcanoes that used to erupt but stopped long ago (Mount Kilimanjaro in Africa is one) are

Sleepy head . . . Since Capulin Volcano is less than 25,000 years old, scientists can't call it extinct. It's possible that Capulin will erupt again. Who knows?

*Hawaii is famous for **shield** volcanoes shaped like a warrior's shield. **Cinder cone** volcanoes, like Capulin Mountain and Sunset Crater, are mound shapes.*

extinct, or dead. If scientists aren't sure about a volcano, they call it **dormant**, or sleeping. Mount Fuji in Japan is snoozing and so is Haleakala in the Hawaiian islands. If you live near a dormant volcano, how would your life change if it suddenly "woke up"?

You wouldn't want to stick your toe into the earth's mantle to test the temperature. Twenty to forty miles below the surface or crust of our planet, your big toe would find **magma**, rock so hot it's liquid, plus rocky material as well as steam and gas. There's lots of pressure, too! When magma erupts from a weak spot in Earth's crust, it's called **lava**. If you've ever had a coke or an orange soda explode from the can, you know something about pressure and eruptions.

Rings of Fire and Grinding Plates

Beneath the surface of the earth, at least seven giant plates are moving around. They are so huge that the continents and oceans rest on top of them. Where one plate bumps against another plate, earthquakes and volcanoes are common events. If you mark a world map with X's for every volcanic eruption, name the marked areas **rings of fire**.

Make Your Own Volcano

You need a soda bottle, a baking pan, baking soda, a cup of vinegar, red food coloring, and dirt. You put the soda bottle in the pan and surround it with a mountain of dirt (keep the bottle clean inside). One tablespoon of baking soda goes into the bottle. Color the vinegar red and pour it into the bottle. Stand back! You should have a volcano erupting by now. When baking soda meets vinegar, the result is carbon dioxide gas.

When there's enough gaseous pressure, the liquid is forced out of the bottle.

CAPULIN VOLCANO NATIONAL MONUMENT, NEW MEXICO

Cccrraaaaakkkkkkkkkkk! Ash and fire exploding into the sky. Kkkbbooooommmmm! Red hot, molten lava flowing like a river. Only 10,000 years ago, Capulin Mountain was actively erupting. When you stand on top of this once-mighty volcano, you can count more than 100 other cinder cone volcanoes in the surrounding countryside. They represent the tail end of 2 million years of a great volcanic period in Earth's history. Now look down at your feet. You're standing on layers of cinder, ash, and other types of rocks that exploded out of Capulin with each eruption. As they fell back to earth, they landed on the main vent and eventually formed the conical mountain below you.

Capulin is an almost perfect conical shape. Lava flowed from subvents located at the western base of the cone, not from the main crater.

First Stop!

When you visit Capulin Volcano National Monument, begin at the **Visitor's Center** for brochures, books, and a red-hot video. People in wheelchairs can cruise the 60-meter (200-foot) nature trail located outside. There's a great stop for picnics and stretching just as you begin your drive up the mountain. Fasten your seat belt for the rest of the ride. Around and around and around you'll go, and the mountainside is very steep! From the top, try to spot three different states in the distance: Texas, Oklahoma, and Colorado.

Look out from the top of Capulin Volcano and try to pick out Cimarron Cut-Off and the site of the **Old Santa Fe Trail**. About 100 years ago, wagon trains used Capulin Mountain as a landmark on their journey to **Fort Union**.

Enter the Volcano

This is one of the few places in the entire world where you can walk straight into a volcano. **Crater Rim Trail** completely circles the volcano rim. It's 1.6 kilometers (1 mile) long, and you might pass mule deer, bluebirds, goldfinches, and occasionally even a rattlesnake along the way. Volcanic soil is very fertile and plants love to grow here. See if you can pick out paintbrush, sunflowers, or lupine growing nearby. Another short trail (.03 kilometer/.02 mile) drops to the bottom of the crater where you can view the vent up close.

Take Time...

When you visit Capulin Volcano National Monument, take time to stop at the rim and close your eyes. What do you hear? Smell? Feel?

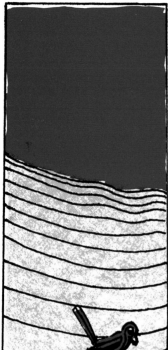

SUNSET CRATER NATIONAL MONUMENT, ARIZONA

Sunset Crater National Monument features a 1,000-foot volcanic cone, the youngest volcano in the state. When Sunset Crater erupted in A.D. 1064-65, the ancient Sinagua peoples were forced to abandon their homes in a hurry.

Start at the **Visitor Center** and ask a ranger about the **ice cave** located along the nature trail. A one-mile hiking trail leads from the base of Sunset Crater and loops through the volcanic moonscape. The brittle lava is **aa** (pronounced ah ah). You'll see an **anosma** (a squeeze-up formation), formed when molten lava squeezes like toothpaste from cracks in the rock.

Who Put the Sunset in Sunset Crater?

Around the year A.D. 1200, Sunset Crater erupted for the final time. The lava shooting from the vents contained sulfur and iron. After the eruption, gases escaped through vents and oxidized the mineral particles. It's as if nature painted a permanent "sunset" on the cone.

Take Time . . .

When you visit Sunset Crater National Monument, take time to notice the plants and animals who live in this strange and wonderful environment.

Some of the Sinagua people who lived near Sunset Crater moved to the area that is now **Wupatki National Monument, Arizona**. *They left behind wonderful multilevel pueblo ruins and a ball court that you may visit today. It's only a hop, skip, and a jump from Sunset Crater.*

5. Beneath the Surface of the Earth

Some people get scared just thinking about caves. Others (especially spelunkers and speleologists) can't wait to climb inside and explore every cranny and crevice of these natural underground chambers. One thing is certain: the more you learn about caves, the less scary they become, and the more fun you can have.

Caves come in different shapes and varieties like lava tube, sandstone, and sea caves. Carlsbad Caverns, Timpanogos Cave, and Lehman Caves at Great Basin National Park are all **limestone solution caves** (water dissolves limestone to create hollow chambers). Before you step inside a cave, close your eyes and think back 200 million years or so, when much of the Southwest region was an inland sea. Sea critters like algae, sponges, and sea snails lived in the shallow, murky water. When they died, they sank to the bottom where bits of dirt, rock, and sand settled on top of them. Calcite, a mineral in the seawater, helped harden these piles of shell and sand into a type of rock called limestone. Eventually, the sea dried up, and everything was covered over with deposits of salts and gypsum (another mineral). About 60 million years ago

(when the last dinosaurs walked the earth), some of the limestone was uncovered by wind and water, and some of it was pushed up by Earth's inner rumblings. As rainwater seeped into cracks and fractures, the limestone began dissolving very sllooowwwwllllllyyyyyy. Eventually, cracks and holes became the amazing caves you can explore today.

Action!

Of course, that's a very simple explanation for a very, very complicated process, and sometimes action will give you a better idea than words. In one week, collect all the sugar cubes you can find. Stack them squarely until you build a sugar cube box. Now, carefully drip water on top. As the water seeps down through the sugar seams, the cubes will dissolve and you'll have your own sticky-sweet cave. In real caves, the dripping water must be slightly acidic to dissolve the limestone. It also takes much longer—like a million years. **Joints**, **partings**, and **faults** (like the seams of the sugar cubes) are some of the types of cracks where the water begins its work in limestone.

Soda Straws, Toadstools, Cave Bacon, and Pearls

These **speleothems** are limestone cave decorations that come in many shapes, sizes, and colors. You'll see faces, lions' tails, cathedrals, monsters, and fairy palaces in the cave formations. When water seeps through cracks in the earth's rock, acid in the water dissolves tiny bits of limestone. Stalactites begin to form when a drop of water leaves a ring of limestone on the cave ceiling. Drop after drop eventually makes a

***Spelunkers** and **speleologists** are not purple spiders, overgrown fish, or designer jeans. Spel—the root—comes from Latin and Greek words meaning "cave." Speleologists are scientists who study cave geology, cave animal life, or cave water systems. Spelunkers explore caves for fun.*

45

hollow soda straw of limestone. If the straw becomes plugged, limestone icicles form on the outside.

When water flows quickly, it drips onto the cave floor and limestone deposits grow toward the ceiling. After thousands of years, mighty stalagmites form. Cave bacon, flowstone, columns, pearls, and crystals are other amazing formations you might see.

Make Your Own Mighty Stalactite!
You can make your own stalactite at home with a few simple ingredients: water, two jars, natural fiber string, cardboard, and epsom salts. Mix up a nice thick solution of salt and water in each jar. With the filled jars placed about six inches apart on the cardboard, soak the string in the salt solution. Now put one end of the string in each jar with enough slack so that it forms a U between the jars. Do not let the string touch the cardboard. Within several days, you should have your own stalactites!

CARLSBAD CAVERNS NATIONAL PARK, NEW MEXICO

Carlsbad Caverns National Park has more than 70 caves already discovered on its 46,755 acres. Some are tiny, and others are humongous. In fact, the **Big Room** in Carlsbad Cavern is 14 acres big. You could fit the Empire State Building and the Astro Dome inside it and still have room to move! **New Cave**, located 23 miles from Carlsbad Cavern near the mouth of **Slaughter Canyon**, is much smaller and is called a wild cave because it's undeveloped. Other caves are so small you must crawl in and out. No one knows how many

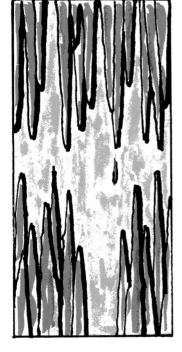

Stalactites and stalagmites are speleothems. Remember: stalagmites need all their "might" to grow upwards from the cave floor, and stalactites must hang "tight."

caves filled with awesome formations remain hidden in the Guadalupe Mountain Range.

Only a few of the park's caves are open to the public. **Carlsbad Cavern** has an elevator that will take you down to the Big Room. People in wheelchairs can maneuver on most of the trails. Some caves can be visited by special permits. Others, like **Lechuguilla Cave**, are for scientific exploration and research only.

Of course, Carlsbad Caverns National Park isn't just about caves. It has a fabulous desert landscape and diverse plant and animal life.

When you visit Carlsbad Caverns National Park, there are lots of ways to spend your time both below and above the ground. You should definitely take a tour of Carlsbad Cavern. And then there's the Nature Trail, a flashlight tour of New Cave, the summer bat flight program, and a scenic desert drive if your feet are tired.

The **Visitor Center** has information, maps, books, displays, and movies. You can make reservations to tour New Cave or grab a bite at the snack bar. You'll brush up on geology, find out about cave helicites, stalactites, and stalagmites. There's also a sleek and shiny hands-on speleothem for you to handle all you want. You aren't allowed to touch any formations in the cavern because the rocks need to be protected from human damage. The oil from your hands will discolor ancient formations, and they're easily broken. Although the cavern is still very beautiful, more than 17,000 formations have been broken during its 60-year history as a national park. It's a federal crime; it's also an ecological one. Those formations took thousands of years to develop, but they can be destroyed in

Lights out! *What does it feel like to be in total darkness? A tour through New Cave or the main cavern during the summer will give you the chance to find out. The rangers turn out the lights for a few minutes, and silence and pitch black are all you hear and see.*

48

just one thoughtless moment. And since the formations' growth has all but ceased, they will never grow back. Treat everything around you with respect, and as the rangers say, take only pictures and memories, and leave only footprints.

Carlsbad Caverns

One of the early explorers of Carlsbad Caverns was a 12-year-old boy with an unusual name. In 1883, Rolth Sublett's father lowered him into the cave to see what he could see. When you walk inside, imagine what it might feel like to be swinging from a rope in darkness, instead of walking on the lighted path.

There are many stories of people who witnessed the bat flights from the mouth of the cavern. Eventually, some enterprising folks began to talk about mining the bat **guano** (excrement), which is rich in nitrates, to fertilize soil. In 1903, buckets were lowered, shafts dug, and mine cars began to transport tons of guano. In fact, in 20 years, more than 100,000 tons of guano were mined!

In early mining years, no one strayed far from the cave entrance except 19-year-old Jim White, who was a very curious miner. On his days off, he explored the deeper caverns with his miner's lantern. Because of his passion and enthusiasm, he convinced others that a vast and awesome wilderness lay hidden underground. In 1923, President Calvin Coolidge proclaimed Carlsbad Caverns a national monument.

*If you were an Indian of the Guadalupe Mountains living about 1,000 years ago, you would have known about **New Cave**. Today, rangers lead visitors on flashlight tours to view fantastic cave formations like the 60-foot-high **Monarch**, the **Christmas Tree**, and the **Chinese Wall**. Tours are by reservation only. Wear sturdy shoes and B.Y.O. canteen and flashlight.*

NATIONAL PARK SERVICE PHOTOGRAPH

JIM WHITE

Jim White became Carlsbad's first chief ranger.

49

Bat Fans

What do a hundred thousand free-tail bats sound like when they're whizzing over your head? A whirlwind? A tidal wave? A school lunchroom?

If you visit Carlsbad Caverns National Park in spring, summer, or fall, you can answer that question with your own ears. You can even make a tape recording or use a video camera (but no flash).

From May through September (in most years), as many as 5,000 bats per minute (or BPM) exit the cavern each day at dusk to begin their nocturnal search for insects and water. That's a lot of bat wings! (During times of severe drought, the numbers of bats are sometimes lower.) Carlsbad

Caverns offers a special **bat flight program** for visitors. While you wait for the bats to take off from the bat cave in the cavern, rangers will give you some fascinating bat facts and answer your bat questions.

If you think bats are just the inspiration for comic books, movies, and vampire fantasies, think again. There are roughly 900 species of bats in the world, 15 of which can be found in Carlsbad Caverns National Park.

Bats are the only mammals that can truly fly. They come in all shapes, colors, and sizes, and their wingspan ranges from 5½ inches to 5½ feet across according to species. Bats are not blind, but most species use sonar or echolocation to maneuver in the dark. Bats send out ultrasonic (high-frequency) sounds through their nose or mouth. When these sounds echo from or bounce off close objects, they are picked up again by the bat's very large ears. This is also how they "echo locate" tiny moving insects in the dark. At Carlsbad Caverns, most of the bats are **Mexican free-tail bats**, named after the construction of their tails and the fact that they migrate to Mexico for the winter.

People love to tell spooky stories about bloodsucking bats that prey on large animals and humans! Those stories may stand your hair on end, but don't confuse them with the real story. Most bats eat insects. In fact, bats play an important role in nature because they help keep the insects from having a population explosion.

It's been estimated that as many as 8 million Mexican free-tail bats may have resided in the main bat cave at Carlsbad Caverns at one time. In one night, that many bats could eat 100,000

*Once a year, the second Thursday in August, from 5 to 7 a.m., a special **Bat Flight Breakfast** is sponsored by park employees. Other visitor activities may include a lantern tour through the cavern and special programs.*

Who goes there? *What types of creatures live in caves? Monsters, giants, and dragons are more likely found in books. Inside a real cave you might find bats, beetles, and crickets especially adapted to darkness. Whatever you find—do not disturb!*

pounds of insects for dinner. For each bat, that equals about one-third their body weight or a bellyful.

After a hard night's work, the bats return to the cave at dawn. If you're an early riser, you'll witness spectacular bat dives from hundreds of feet at speeds of 25 mph or more. One look and you'll be a bat fan forever.

Take Time . . .
On your visit to Carlsbad Caverns National Park, take time to learn about cave insects. They live in total darkness and they have adapted to "nightlife."

TIMPANOGOS CAVE NATIONAL MONUMENT, UTAH

Enter at the Grotto. After many paces, stop at Father Time Jewel Box and then continue to the Cavern of Sleep. After a wink or two, proceed to Hidden Lake, and finally, marvel at the Great Heart of Timpanogos.

Sound like a treasure hunt? You're right. These are all nature's treasures, and you'll find them at Timpanogos Cave National Monument.

Discover fabulous stalactites and stalagmites, shimmering aragonite crystals, and white helictites like rock candy. Even though they look good enough to eat, don't taste or touch. Remember, it took thousands of years for these wonders to form. Ask your ranger about the special stalagmites that you *are* supposed to touch.

Cave tours are very popular, and you must sign up at the **Visitors Center** before you walk up to the caves. Take some time to learn all about weird and fascinating cave formations, how caves are made, and the stories of American Fork

Canyon and the mountains that surround you. Next door, pick up munchies for the hike, souvenirs, film, and flashbulbs (you'll need them for cave photos).

Identified Flying Geology!
American Fork Canyon is a new kid on the geologic block. The natural forces that make a canyon—wind and water erosion, freezing and thawing, and other organic action—are still very much at work. Nature is on the job 24 hours a day, and "building a canyon" creates falling rocks. That means you may have to duck for cover as you travel the trail to the caves. A blue stripe painted on the trail means you're in an area especially prone to rolling rocks. Keep moving! Most flying objects are as small as a tennis ball, but they can give you a big headache. Keep your ears open for rumbling or crashing sounds; you'll hear before you see. Duck for cover near the inside of the trail and protect your head with your arms. When all is quiet, proceed on your way.

Tour de Force (of Nature, That Is!)
It's a whole different world underground: the darkness, the moisture, the smells, the living creatures. It might not be that different from the way some people imagine far planets in outer space might be.

To visit the incredible limestone caves, first you must climb a mile and a half up Timpanogos, a 3,660-meter (12,000-foot) mountain in Utah's **Wasatch Range**. Huff and puff? Maybe, but once you reach your destination, wow!

After you enter **Hansen Cave** at the Grotto, the

Have you ever seen a rainbow made of rock? Cave formations would be just plain white if it weren't for minerals that mix with your basic-cave-formation-ingredient, calcite. Iron oxide supplies the browns, reds, and oranges. Nickel gives us yellow. Pink is courtesy of manganese. And nickel magnesium silicate (a mouthful) is lime green. Thanks, guys!

Crystal Palace! Assemble one pie tin, one large bowl, a few bits of charcoal, ½ cup each of water, liquid bluing, and salt, 1 cup ammonia, food coloring (blue, green, or yellow), and a spoon. Fill the pie tin with a charcoal crust. Mix water, bluing, ammonia, and salt (Yuck!) in the bowl and pour over charcoal. Careful! Top with a few squirts of food coloring. Let sit overnight. Do you see the crystals growing!

ranger will guide you for a half-mile (about one hour's worth) through **Middle Cave** and, finally, **Timpanogos Cave**. Passing from one cave to the next is managed via man-made tunnels that were built in the 1930s. Why do you think it's cold inside a cave? It might remind you of a refrigerator because the temperature stays pretty constant. That has to do with all that rock insulating you.

Hansen Cave was discovered in 1887 by Martin Hansen. He was hot on the trail of a cougar whose tracks led to the cave entrance. Middle Cave and Timpanogos Cave weren't discovered until 1921. These caves are small, but they're jam-packed with awesome formations. Weird helictites abound in **Chimes Chamber**, and the **Great Heart of Timpanogos** is a huge formation made of several stalactites "holding hands."

Take Time . . .

On your visit to Timpanogos Cave National Monument, take time to touch a stalagmite. The ranger will show you two stalagmites made just for touching. Get all your feelies out on these; see if they feel like anything else you've ever touched.

GREAT BASIN NATIONAL PARK, NEVADA

Caves and glaciers. You'll discover both at Great Basin National Park. Wheeler Peak boasts the Great Basin's only glacier. At the time of the last Ice Age, ice covered much of the North American continent, and glaciers scraped and scoured the mountains.

Caves take thousands and thousands of years

to form, and glaciers take ages to create their mountainous sculptures, but Great Basin National Park is a youngster. It was created in 1986. Lehman Caves National Monument was combined with national forest land to give us a new national park where you can explore varied plant and animal habitats, from the Upper Sonoran Desert communities to the Arctic Alpine tundra life zone.

The **Visitor Center**, next to Lehman Caves, is where you should start the day. A slide show will tell you about the entire park, and a brief film concentrates on Lehman Caves and limestone cave formation. There are displays to explore and books, souvenirs, and snacks to buy.

For a short, sweet, and informative glimpse of the natural world surrounding you, try the **Visitor Center Nature Trail**. At ¼ mile, it's an easy warm-up for later hikes, and you'll learn about the plants, wildlife, and geology of the area.

Happy Trails to You

If you or your boots are in the mood for a hike, get ready, get set, get smart; carry water, wear sturdy shoes, take a grown-up along, and pace yourself. This is high altitude hiking, and you need to take it slower than usual.

Lehman Creek Trail (4 miles) is a challenge! If you begin at Upper Lehman Creek Campground, you'll gain 2,150 feet by the time you reach Wheeler Creek Campground. The trail follows Lehman Creek and gives you a varied look at area life zones—from desert piñon/juniper to Arctic Alpine tundra. You may also reverse the hike and start at Wheeler Creek Campground for a downhill trip.

Heat wave! The earth is about 9 degrees warmer than it was during the last Ice Age and it's getting warmer still. Scientists predict another 5 degree increase in world temperatures by the year 2030. This global warming is probably caused by natural planetary cycles combined with worldwide pollution, loss of world forests, and too many people. For whatever reason, a warmer earth means you might not be able to see Wheeler Peak Glacier in 20 to 40 years because it may have melted away.

Lexington Arch is a 6-story limestone arch that was probably part of an underground passageway long ago. It takes a bumpy drive on a dirt road and a one-mile hike on the trail to get there. It's worth it!

Baker Creek Trail will lead you along Baker Creek to lovely Baker Lake. You're at 10,630 feet (wow!), so take it easy. This trail starts where Baker Creek Road ends just six-tenths of a mile above the campground. On the trail, check out the wondrous diversity of plant communities. Just like your hometown, all types of "plant peoples" live here.

Alpine Lake Loop Trail is a fairly easy way to visit two alpine lakes. Beginning at Wheeler Peak Campground, the 3-mile loop winds past Stella and Teresa lakes.

Wonderground Underland

Lehman Caves is that old friend, a limestone solution cave. One thing is always the same for every limestone cave: they're all different. Cave formations are a wonderful way to appreciate the incredible diversity of nature.

Early Native Americans knew of Lehman Caves, but it wasn't officially discovered until 1885 when a local rancher and miner, Absalom S. Lehman, ventured inside. He was probably the first person to really explore the caves—almost 1½ miles worth of underground passages. Lehman also led others through the caves—800 curious pioneers, who were amazed by the wonderland of stalactites, stalagmites, flowstone, and even the very rare limestone **shields**. Only about one percent of the world's caves have shield formations. Imagine a crack in the rock where pres-

On the Move! *Glaciers are made when so much snow piles up during winter that it doesn't all melt in summer. After a while, the weight of the snow is so heavy that some of it compresses into ice. Glaciers don't stop there; they move slowly down mountains making a giant sculpture as they go.*

sure forces the water out and crystals form along the edges of the crack. This process repeats itself until two disks are formed. The stalactites that hang from the edges of the shields add to the magic.

Today's well-marked trail covers ½ mile and includes six stairways. A ranger will share lots of great information and answer questions on the 1½-hour tour. You'll pass through the **Gothic Palace** to the **Grand Palace** where the ceiling looks like the underside of a vegetable garden— onions, turnips, carrots, parsnips, and potatoes made of calcite.

Oh Pine, Oh Cone

Pinus longaeva is not a fancy pasta, it's the scientific name for the incredible Great Basin bristlecone pine. Among the oldest trees in the world, they're growing all around you in the park. These awesome trees can grow to be more than 4,000 years old!

Some bristlecone pines grow at lower elevations where water is plentiful and the soil is rich. These don't live as long as the bristlecone pines that grow at elevations over 9,000 feet. This was a puzzle for scientists, and they studied the annual growth rings of the trees. At lower elevations, the rings were widely spaced and the wood was not as dense as trees growing at high elevations. Scientists believe the denser wood from higher-elevation trees is more resistant to disease and weather than lower-elevation trees.

Take Time . . .

While you're visiting Great Basin National Park, take time to participate in a ranger-guided walk or talk.

When the living is easy, the bristlecone pine grows like regular trees. But in years (and areas) of hardship, this smart tree dies back until just enough living tree is left to match the available water and nutrients in the earth.

6. First People

Atlatl the who? *Before the introduction of the bow and arrow, this handy spear was used by the Basketmakers for hunting and defense.*

It happened a very long time ago compared to your next birthday, but in terms of Earth's 4½ billion birthdays, it's only yesterday. At the end of the last great Ice Age (about 15,000 years ago), some scientists believe that prehistoric people walked on their own two feet all the way from Asia to North and South America. That's a very long haul, especially without hiking boots! These hunters kept on trekking, following herds of elk, reindeer, and other wild game.

These first people are probably the ancestors of the **Anasazi** and maybe even all American Indians. The Anasazi lived in what is now the American Southwest from somewhere in the first century to A.D. 1300. *Anasazi* is a Navajo word that can translate as "the ancient ones." No one knows what the Anasazi called themselves; they left behind no books, poems, or shopping lists when they disappeared. Archaeologists have discovered ancient baskets, pottery, petroglyphs (rock carvings), and other clues to this great culture. Although there are still many mysteries to solve, it's clear they were smart, energetic, and creative people.

Who, What, When?

Anasazi history can be divided into two basic groups, the **Basketmaker** and the **Pueblo**. You can probably guess why archaeologists call the first Anasazi Early Basketmakers. They used baskets to hold food, water, and anything else that needed holding. They lived in caves, simple shelters, and pit houses. It was a fairly mobile life based on hunting, limited corn crops, and wild plants. This went on for several hundred years as they were exposed to new ideas and skills.

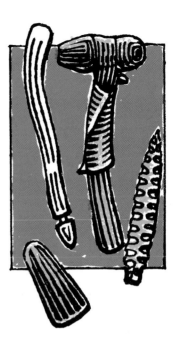

By the year 500, some Anasazi began settling into a more permanent life-style that included farming, durable homes, and religious ceremonies. Two hundred years later, they had discovered their own versions of "high-tech" tools like the bow and arrow and the full-grooved ax. And by A.D. 900, they were constructing a different style of house that earned them the name Pueblos. These stone "apartments" sometimes rose four stories high and held hundreds of people. What do you think daily life was like in the Anasazi pueblos? How do you begin to find out?

It's a Date!

Archaeologists use several techniques to figure out who did what and when. One is **carbon-14 dating** and another is a mouthful, **dendrochronology**. Carbon-14 has nothing to do with Saturday nights. Instead, it's a source of natural radiation in all living organisms. After something dies, it gives off less and less radiation. Scientists can measure exact amounts of

radiation and come up with the approximate date something was alive.

Dendrochronology sounds like a wizard who lives at the center of the world, but actually, it is the study of tree rings. Trees are very sensitive to their environment. Each year they add a new layer or ring to their trunk. If you know the age of one tree and compare it with another and another and another, you can count back thousands of years. What does all this have to do with prehistoric people? The Anasazi used logs (the trunks of trees) to support their pueblos, and scientists use dendrochronology to date the logs!

The Mystery of the Disappearing People

The year is A.D. 1300 and many of the great pueblos are now home to desert winds, snakes, rabbits, and insects. Why did the Anasazi leave? Did the water dry up? Were they raided by enemies? No one has solved the mystery for certain, but scientific evidence supports both theories. A drought covered much of the Southwest at the time of the disappearance, and nomadic raiding

tribes began to roam the area. For whatever reason, these great people left with barely a trace.

Many Cultures

Zuñi, Hopi, Navajo, Apache, and Pueblo are a few of the many Indian cultures you might visit in the American Southwest. Some Indian peoples, like the Hopi and the Zuñi, may be descendants of the Anasazi.

When you travel on tribal land, be considerate and respectful of other people's customs and way of life. They might be very different from your own.

Navajo believe it is rude to look another person in the eye. Many Indian cultures believe it is rude to point your finger. People's homes are private property; do not enter without an invitation. Videos, photography, tape recordings, and sketching are prohibited on all reservations unless you receive special permission.

A journey to different Indian nations is a great way to appreciate other peoples' life-styles, religions, architecture, arts, and crafts.

Squaaakkkkk! How did parrots and shell beads get to Chaco Canyon? Chaco Anasazi were very busy traders. Parrots were valued for beautiful bright feathers. They were most certainly brought from Mexico. Shell beads came from Mexico or California.

CHACO CANYON NATIONAL HISTORICAL PARK, NEW MEXICO

In medieval Europe, William the Conquerer ordered builders to begin constructing the Tower of London; in Spain, El Cid was storming the city of Valencia to take it from the Moors. In the San Juan Basin, Anasazi peoples were thriving in communities at Chaco Canyon—the area that is now Chaco Canyon National Historical Park.

The weather at Chaco is about the same now as it was a thousand years ago—cold and windy winters and hot, hot, hot summers. It might seem a strange place for the Anasazi to settle, but settle they did. They flourished, too!

They planted beans, corn, and squash on the lowlands, built amazing 3- and 4-story pueblos of sandstone and mud mortar, and constructed more than 400 miles of desert roads connecting 75 different communities.

Chaco Canyon National Historical Park is a fabulous place to explore the mysteries of Anasazi culture. You can wander through ruins, hike onto clifftops, camp under sandstone bluffs, and have excellent adventures.

To find out where to begin, start at the **Visitor Center**. You'll find museum exhibits showing a great model of Anasazi village life, movies, books, maps, a rest room, and water. It's very dry out here, so don't forget to fill your canteen before you begin to explore.

Pretty Village

At **Pueblo Bonito**, hop into your time machine once more and set the dial back 1,000 years. Step out into the plaza or center courtyard of this

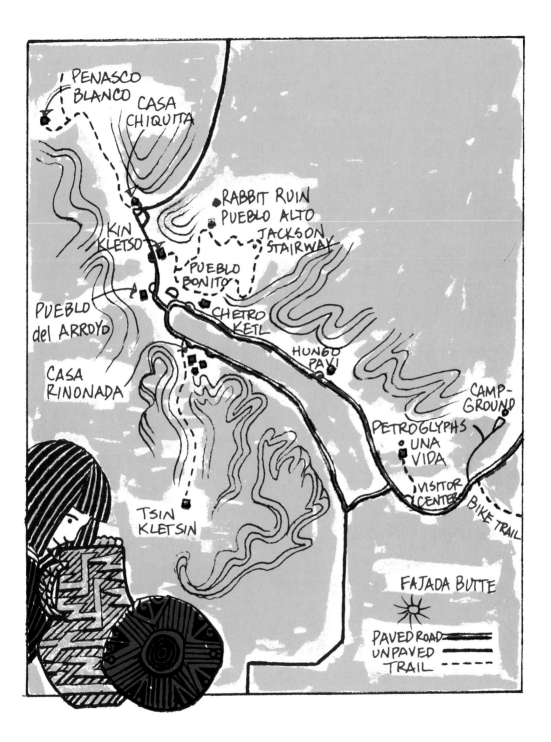

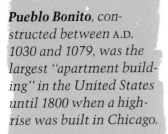

Pueblo Bonito, con-
structed between A.D.
1030 and 1079, was the
largest "apartment build-
ing" in the United States
until 1800 when a high-
rise was built in Chicago.

pueblo. Notice the women husking and shelling corn. There's a girl making a clay pot, and a young boy is scraping a rabbit hide with a deer-bone tool.

Wander around the plaza and look into the small rooms where you hear the sound of corn being ground on metates (large, flat grinding stones).

Nearby, in the large kiva (round underground rooms used as religious centers), several men are weaving, spinning, and carving tools. Now you pass ground-floor rooms filled with grain, beans, squash, and wild berries to be eaten during the winter months.

Peer through a doorway and you'll see an old man resting near a firepit, while outside two children are playing stickball with a carved tree branch and a round stone. As you look up, many families are busily working in the apartments rising four stories over your head.

Walking behind the pueblo, you notice a giant rock cracked away from the cliffs, propped up with wooden posts and rocks dangerously near pueblo walls.

Now fiddle with your dials and return to the present. **Threatening Rock** has become a jumble of broken stones in a pile between the cliffs and the pueblo ruins. In the last 900 years, the rock and the ruins have crumbled, but archaeology and our imagination allow us to discover the past.

High on Hiking
Ask park rangers about the narrow trail that climbs up the face of the cliffs behind Pueblo

Bonito and leads to ancient ruins and roads on the mesa top. Take along water and a grown-up and wear hiking boots or tennis shoes. Once on top, you'll feel almost as high as the ravens flying around you. Don't go too close to the edge of the cliff, but **do** check out the incredible view of the San Juan Basin and the other pueblos you can visit.

What's in a Name?

Una Vida is closest to the Visitor Center, and it will give you an idea of how all the ruins looked before they were excavated. The Spanish name means "one life," but no one is sure why it was called this. The Navajo names for this pueblo are *asdzaa halgoni bighan*, "witchcraft woman's home," and *astohalkoi bikin*, "house of the woman who makes you thin by starving you." You'll find petroglyphs nearby.

Fajada Butte is named for the band (*fajada*) of lignite coal that you see halfway up the butte.

Chetro Ketl has about 500 rooms and 16 kivas. No one remembers the meaning or origin of this name, but the Navajos also call it *nastl 'a kin*, "house in a corner."

Casa Rinconada ("Canyon House" in Spanish) is a very large kiva that you can climb down into.

Tsin Kletsin means "Black Wood" and might be named for burned timbers discovered here. It will probably take you about 30 or 45 minutes to hike to Tsin Kletsin. Bring water and watch out for loose rocks and rattlesnakes.

Pueblo Alto, on top of the mesa, was an ancient crossroads. Hike up, and you'll understand why it's called "High Village" in Spanish.

Sun Signs

Was it a shrine honoring the sun? Was it a calendar marking the days to plant, tend, and harvest the crops? No one is absolutely sure what purpose the **Fajada Butte Solstice Marker** served, but it was very important to the Chaco Anasazi.

High on a cliff near the top of Fajada Butte, three sheets of rock stand facing two spiral petroglyphs. During spring and fall equinox and winter and summer solstice, a dagger-shaped sunbeam marks the spirals.

Because the area of the marker is fragile, you aren't allowed to hike up. This will help ensure that the marker exists for future scientific study and use in Native American religious rituals.

Take Time . . .

While visiting Chaco Canyon, if you camp overnight, take time to count the stars and listen to the coyotes howl.

CANYON DE CHELLY NATIONAL MONUMENT, ARIZONA

Step Lightly

Imagine yourself crossing a vast desert under a blazing sun. As you walk, you watch the rain clouds gather over distant mountains and you daydream about a drink of cool water. Your eye is on one special bird-shaped cloud as you step over a red sandstone rock, but you look down just in time to stop yourself from walking into thin air. Your heart pounds like a drum as you stare 1,000 feet into the magnificent canyon below.

That might be just how the earliest visitors discovered Canyon de Chelly—by surprise. For at least 2,000 years, people have been living in the canyon. Long ago, the Anasazi carved pictures on the red rocks, grew corn, and wove baskets. Today, Navajo people farm and graze livestock in the bottom of the canyon, just as their families have done for about 300 years.

Now there are railed lookouts, horseback tours, 6-wheel truck tours, and a foot trail into Canyon de Chelly. Still, most of what you see today looks like it did 2,000 years ago. That might not seem so amazing until you think about your hometown. How did it look 2,000 years ago? What are some of the ways we can live in balance with nature and lightly on the land?

Tribal Lands

Canyon de Chelly is the only monument within the National Park Service located entirely on Navajo tribal land where the Navajo continue to live and work. The two main canyons (**Canyon de Chelly** and **Canyon del Muerto**) are sacred to

Most people say Canyon de Chelly as in "dah SHAY." De Chelly stems from tsegi *(tsay yih), the Navajo word for "rock canyon." During 200 years of Spanish and English mispronunciation, "tsay yih" slowly became "dah SHAY."*

Canyon de Chelly National Monument, located entirely on Navajo tribal land, was officially established in 1931. It was approved by the Federal Government and the Navajo Tribal Council, which is the governing body of the Navajo Nation.

Time out! The Navajo Nation is on daylight saving time from about April 2 to October 28. All the rest of Arizona (including the Hopi Reservation) is on mountain standard time. So keep an eye on your watch.

Navajo people. They also contain important prehistoric and historic archaeological sites, petroglyphs, and pictographs. Treat the canyons with respect, and don't forget, people still live here!

You may hike on White House Trail, but other trips into the canyons must always be taken with authorized guides. You can and should let your imagination run wild.

Canyon Cruises

Before you take a canyon cruise, stop at the **Visitor Center** to find out about horseback rides, nature programs, and how to become a **Jr. Ranger**.

The upper and lower **White House** ruins are located about six miles up the main canyon from the Visitor Center. You can reach them by guided jeep tour, horseback tour, or on foot via the White House Trail. This ruin is named for a white plaster wall in the upper cave portion.

Antelope House in Canyon del Muerto is only reached by guided jeep or horseback tours. This pueblo had 40 or 50 rooms built at the base of a towering cliff. When you see four tan and white antelopes painted on a cliff, you'll understand the name. Local Navajo believe these were painted by Dibe Yazhi (Little Sheep), a Navajo artist who painted here in the 1830s. The pictographs painted in solid white were probably drawn by Anasazi.

Massacre Cave (also in Canyon del Muerto) was named for the 1645 battle between Spanish Lieutenant Antonio Narbona's troops and Navajo Indians. The Spanish killed many Indian men, women, and children but reported their own losses at only one dead and 64 wounded.

A Thousand Words

Standing Cow Ruin received its name because of a wonderful blue-headed cow painted on it by a Navajo artist.

On a nearby cliff, a timeless procession of soldiers march across the rock face on horseback. They probably record a nineteenth-century Spanish expedition.

Can you guess why these can't be prehistoric pictographs? Because horses were not seen in this area until the Spanish brought them to America in the 1500s.

White House Trail begins at White House Overlook. Take two hours, good shoes, and water. In winter, snow and ice may cover the trail. Do stay on the trail to avoid disturbing canyon residents.

Take Time . . .
At Canyon de Chelly, take time to lie down on sandstone and gaze at clouds.

MESA VERDE NATIONAL PARK, COLORADO

What if the year is 2095 and future kids are visiting the abandoned ruins of the town where you live right now? What questions will they ask, and what will they look for?

They might wonder what you were like. How did you spend your days? Did you work? What tools did you have, and what games did you play? And where did you go when your family and friends disappeared?

When you visit Mesa Verde National Park, you'll probably wonder those very same things about the families who lived here a thousand

In 1887, Virginia McClurg began a political campaign to convince Americans and members of Congress to protect and preserve the Mesa Verde cliff dwellings. She gave speeches, wrote articles and poems, and gained the support of more than 250,000 women. She also negotiated with Wiminuche Ute Chief Ignacio so that the ruins would be protected and the Utes would retain grazing rights. Mesa Verde became a national park in 1906.

years ago. Many of your questions will be answered during your visit, but others will remain a mystery for you to ponder.

Secret Cities
Park Headquarters at **Chapin Mesa** is open year-round. **Far View Visitor Center** operates only during summer months. Begin at one or the other, and rangers will answer questions about guided tours, bicycle rentals, and special programs.

The archaeological museum at Chapin Mesa takes you back to the past. The dioramas re-create scenes of everyday Anasazi life. How different is your life today?

Far View Visitor Center has contemporary Indian arts and crafts on display, and free bus tours of **Wetherill Mesa** begin here.

VIRGINIA McCLURG

Cliff Palace is the biggest cliff dwelling with 217 rooms, 25 kivas, and space for 250 people. There are beautiful wall paintings here.

You turkey! Anasazis raised only dogs and turkeys. All other animals were wild. Turkey feathers could be woven into warm blankets and dog hair spun into yarn. Also, both are edible.

In summer, rangers conduct guided tours through several cliff dwellings. Sign up early at the visitor center or museum because these are popular.

In winter, tours go to **Spruce Tree House** only. Two short hiking trails lead into **Spruce Tree Canyon**. Always register at the chief ranger's office before you hike! These are both 10-kilometer (6-mile) loops where you may guide yourself. Bring a grown-up (and binoculars if possible—you have chances to view cliff dwellings from various overlooks). Picnic sites and rest rooms are located along both loops.

At Chapin Mesa, **Balcony House** is the only major ruin that you can't see from a canyon over-look. A ranger-guided tour is only for the brave! This pueblo was built high in the cliffs for defense. There is only one way in and out. You must slip through tight cracks and crevices and then climb a very steep ladder. It's an exciting (and slightly scary) adventure.

If you take a bus to Wetherill Mesa, you'll visit

Long House and **Step House**. At Step House, look for the large boulder used to shape *manos*, the hand stones for grinding grain on metates.

Tips: Always wear sturdy shoes with good traction, step with caution near cliff rims, and don't throw rocks!!!

Overnights
Morefield Campground is a fun way to spend a night or two or three during summer months. Mule deer often come to visit at dusk. Enjoy, but do not share your dinner! You might think you're being generous, but feeding wild animals can cause harm (even death) to you and them.

Take Time . . .
While visiting Mesa Verde, take time to think about the people who lived here so long ago.

BANDELIER NATIONAL MONUMENT, NEW MEXICO
The many ancient cliff dwellings at Bandelier National Monument are "kid sized." Ancient Indians were not large people, and they built small rooms and doors to conserve heat and energy. You'll also find ladders to climb and tight squeezes between cracks and crevices. Besides wonderful ruins, the natural beauty of Frijoles Canyon (Bean Canyon) will knock your socks off. You can camp, hike, visit a ceremonial cave, see the restored Talus House, and let your imagination go wild!

Start at the **Visitors Center** to find out about campfire programs, guided tours, and wilderness permits. You can watch a slide show and view exhibits to learn more about the history of the area.

Solar energy isn't a new idea. The Anasazi used solar energy to warm up Cliff Palace, Square Tower House, Spruce Tree, Buzzard House, Spring House, and Long House. They all faced south or southwest to make the most of winter sun.

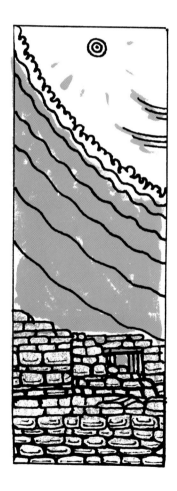

Recycle that trash! Sanitation and what to do with trash was even a problem for ancient folks at Mesa Verde. They had no plumbing or garbage pick-up. In winter, they sometimes used abandoned rooms as toilets and they threw their trash over the front slope. Of course, they didn't have plastic, glass, metal, or newspapers to worry about.

A **loop trail** leads you through the main **Frijoles Canyon ruins**. The hike takes about one hour.

Tsankawi (a separate section of the monument) is a large, unexcavated ruin on a high mesa. The views are fabulous, and the two-mile hike follows an ancient Indian trail that's 18 inches deep in some areas, just from the tread of many feet!

Take Time...
While visiting Bandelier National Monument, take time to attend a campfire lecture and learn something new under the stars.

7. New Worlds

In the early sixteenth century, after Spain conquered Mexico, Spanish explorers heard stories of seven golden cities to the north. These cities were called Cibola. Dreams of great wealth led the Spaniards into the areas that are now Texas and New Mexico. The cities turned out to be the six villages of the Zuñi Indians whose streets were not paved with gold.

Explorers and soldiers were followed by priests who established missions to convert Indians to the Catholic religion. Although many Indians did not want a new religion (both priests and Indians died in the conflict), the Catholic church persisted. Today, many religions in the Southwest use both Native American and Catholic ritual.

EL MORRO NATIONAL MONUMENT, NEW MEXICO

El Morro National Monument is a sandstone bluff rising 200 feet above the valley. This great landmark is also called "Inscription Rock," because of the old "graffiti" that marks it—a register of Indians, Spaniards, and soldiers who were here.

Carved petroglyphs are the work of ancient

Zuñi. A ruin, partly unexcavated, can be seen on the very top of El Morro.

Fifteen years before Pilgrims landed on Plymouth Rock, the first Spaniards carved their inscription on El Morro. The last Spanish inscription dates to 1774.

Explore

Stop at the **Visitors Center** to talk to rangers about your visit. You'll find a hands-on display of animal bones, a snake's skin, arrowheads, and other surprises. There is a digging box outside where you can practice your archaeology, and a grinding stone (metate) with a supply of corn. Go to it! Don't miss the **self-guided hike** that follows the base of the cliff and then climbs to the mesa top. Pick out inscriptions as you go. Imagine what it was like to live on the mesa many years ago.

El Morro has a small picnic and camping area for your enjoyment. Remember, the desert is

famous for unpredictable weather. Watch out for falling rocks, and don't forget the elevation is 7,000 feet. You might run out of breath!

Sign Here!
Of course, you can't sign your name on El Morro. This is a national monument where everything is protected and preserved. But it's fun to follow a time line of inscriptions.

Spaniard Juan de Oñate stopped at El Morro and wrote about the Sea of the South in 1605. Can you find it?

Spanish General Don Diego de Vargas wrote about the Spanish reconquest in 1692. See it?

American army officers cruised by here in 1849. Look for Lt. J. H. Simpson's name.

Take Time . . .
On your visit to El Morro National Monument, take time to think about the people who were here before you. What did they dream of? What made them sad? What brought them happiness?

SAN ANTONIO MISSIONS NATIONAL HISTORIC PARK, TEXAS
In 1492, Spanish explorer Christopher Columbus sailed west from Spain and discovered the "New World." Then he sailed on to claim what are now the West Indies, the Philippines, South America, Central America, Mexico, and the American Southwest for Ferdinand and Isabella, the king and queen of Spain. Other Spanish explorers, conquistadores (soldiers), and priests followed Columbus into this "new" Spain.

Catholic missions were an important part of Spain's efforts to colonize the new world and convert native populations to a Spanish way of

*Near Mission Espada, you can view the 2-centuries-old **Espada Aqueduct** (one of the oldest in the United States). Indians built the 15-mile network of acequias (ditches) and aqueducts that carried water to fields for irrigation.*

life. In some ways, the mission system exploited Indians, who were forced to adapt to a different religion and culture, but it also meant that many ideas were exchanged. Eventually, a new way of life evolved—new foods, ceremonies and rituals, crafts, and art forms—which blended two very different cultures. That way of life still exists in much of the Southwest today.

San Antonio Missions National Historic Park is your chance to visit a national park that is located within a city. This park is really four separate missions in different areas of San Antonio. **Missions Concepción, San José, San Juan**, and **Espada** date back to the 1700s and are connected by the **Mission Trail.** You may travel the trail by car or city bus, but do plan your route in advance to avoid confusion.

Take Time . . .

On your visit to the San Antonio Missions, take time to think about mission life—what it must have been like when the bells chimed and the day began almost three hundred years ago.

8. Westward Ho!

The sun bakes the earth until it cracks beneath your feet and dust rises to your knees like a brown fog. You hear the ching-ching of ox chains, the leathery creak of the harness, and the tharumppooo of the wagon wheels. Your stomach rumbles from hunger and your mouth feels dry as cotton. How many months has it been since you left Independence, Missouri? You were a greenhorn back then before you turned 16. Since that time, you've helped mend wagons, clothes, and even broken bones. You feel a tired pride as you snap the buckskin "poppers" at the tip of the 5-pound whip and holler at the oxen to "move along noooowwwww!" Suddenly, all around you people are yelling and waving their hats in the air. It takes you a moment to make out the cause of the ruckus—up ahead, as small as an anthill, is the welcome sight of Fort Union!

In 1848, the Mexican War ended and the present states of New Mexico, Arizona, Nevada, Utah, California, and parts of Colorado and Wyoming were added to United States territory. One year later, gold was discovered in California and the westward rush was on.

It's mine! As settlers moved west, they laid claim to land that had been the homeland of Apaches, Utes, Comanches, and other Indian tribes for centuries. Fierce wars between Indians and non-Indians lasted for years. Eventually, treaties declared that certain lands, or reservations, belonged to each tribe. Sadly, the government broke its treaty agreements, and many Indians died because of cruel hardships.

Forty-niners, traders, and immigrants of all ages followed trails like the San Antonio-El Paso Road, the Butterfield Overland Trail, and the Santa Fe Trail. These routes cut through Indian country, so the U.S. Army established military posts like Fort Union and Fort Davis to protect travelers from hostile Indian warriors fighting to defend their homeland.

FORT UNION NATIONAL MONUMENT, NEW MEXICO

The wonderful "ghost fort" you see today at Fort Union National Monument is the ruin of the third Fort Union, which dates back to 1863. It took five years to build, and then it was the biggest fort in the entire territory. It included the military post as well as a quartermaster depot with warehouses, shops, corrals, offices and quarters, and an ordnance depot. For almost 30 years, this fort served as a base for troops who fought Indians, tracked outlaws, and protected the supply depot.

The first Fort Union was established in 1851. It was a base for military troops and also a way station or "rest stop" for travelers along the Santa Fe Trail. During the 1850s, soldiers battled with Indians.

The American Civil War began in April 1861 and regular troops were withdrawn from Fort Union and replaced by volunteers. Colonel Edward R. S. Canby was in charge of protecting the area, and he was sure Confederate troops would invade New Mexico. To strengthen defenses, he ordered the construction of the second Fort Union, a strange star-shaped earthwork. As it turned out, the star fort did not get much use.

The Confederate invasion was stopped before it ever reached the star fort. In March 1862, a regiment of Colorado volunteer soldiers (from Fort Union) defeated the Confederate troops at the Battle of Glorieta Pass (40 kilometers/25 miles) southeast of Santa Fe, New Mexico. The Confederates retreated to Texas and the star fort was abandoned.

You're in the Army Now!

Bugle calls were a noisy and important part of a soldier's life. At Fort Union in 1882, reveille sounded at 6:00 a.m., and bugle calls continued throughout the day every thirty to sixty minutes. There was Breakfast Call, Drill Call, Fatigue Call, assembly of guard detail, Dinner Call, First Sergeants Call, Retreat, and even Bed Check at 9:05 p.m. When you visit Fort Union today, you'll hear those same calls just as Fort Union residents did one hundred years ago. Oh, yes, one thing is very different; now they're prerecorded.

Living History

Life at Fort Union was probably very different from what you might imagine. Only a few soldiers rode horses. Some soldiers rode mules, but most traveled on their own two feet. The army issued clothes, food, canteens, guns, and anything else they thought a soldier needed. The **Visitor Center** at Fort Union will give you a chance to look closely at antique army issue items like a canteen, haversack, and tin cup, meat can, and a soldier's shoe. There are antique firearms on display, too.

The scale model of Fort Union as it was in

Soldiers were only one part of Fort Union life—entire families lived on the post. Soldiers' wives often worked as laundresses, cleaning soldiers' uniforms, to earn extra money. Children went to school and did chores just like you. What kinds of games do you think they played?

1876 lets you put the quartermaster depot, the prison, company stables, laundress's quarters, ice house, and parade ground into perspective.

From Memorial Day through Labor Day, Fort Union has a **Living History** program. Park rangers and volunteers dress in period clothing, demonstrate daily activities, and answer your questions. You might find a laundress, complete with tent and washbuckets, or talk to a soldier, or you might see a firing demonstration (using high-quality replicas of antique guns).

FORT DAVIS NATIONAL HISTORIC SITE, TEXAS

In 1849, gold was discovered in California, and many people went west to seek their fortunes. In West Texas, main trails passed through Apache and Comanche country, and the army built forts to protect stagecoaches, wagon trains, and the mail. One of these was called Fort Davis, after Secretary of War Jefferson Davis.

From 1854 to 1891, Fort Davis remained active (except for the Civil War years). Today, roughly a hundred years after the last soldier rode away, one of the best examples of a southwestern frontier military post is yours to discover at Fort Davis National Historic Site.

The **Visitor Center** is located in a restored barracks. Check out exhibits and a slide show of the fort's history. Outside, keep your ears open for the recorded sound of an 1875 Dress Retreat Parade.

In summer, the **Living History** program means park rangers and volunteers will be dressed as soldiers, officers' wives, and servants. Feel free to ask them questions about life at Fort Davis.

You're supposed to! Check at the Visitor Center for a schedule of ranger-guided tours and special programs. And pay your fee!

Buffalo Soldiers at Fort Davis

From 1867 to 1885, Fort Davis was occupied primarily by troops of the Ninth and Tenth U.S. Cavalry and the Twenty-fourth and Twenty-fifth U.S. Infantry. These were black regiments commanded by white officers. The American Civil War was over. Slavery was abolished, but prejudice continued. Black soldiers rarely became officers. Even so, the black regiments became famous for their skill and bravery as soldiers. Tragically, they were assigned to Western Frontier duty where another "civil war" was in progress—the nineteenth-century Indian Wars.

Although they were enemies, Indians named the black soldiers "Buffalo Soldiers" out of respect.

Take Time...

While you're visiting Fort Davis National Monument, take time to learn about history. When we understand the mistakes we made in the past, we do not have to repeat them.

PIPE SPRING NATIONAL MONUMENT, ARIZONA

You probably guessed that Pipe Spring National Monument is located on the site of a natural spring. After the Civil War, Americans continued to expand westward toward the "Great American Desert." Although this arid land could not be farmed, there was enough grass to graze cattle. Texas longhorns, descendants of Spanish

A cowboy's partner was his horse. Good cow ponies had to be smart, strong, and quick. Ponies learned their business for years before they were "the best."

cows, were hearty and "mean" enough to survive life on these rangelands. There was a demand for beef in the East. The only question was how to get the cattle to market. Railroads were part of the answer; and so were cowboys.

A visit to Pipe Spring is a chance to relive some of those cowboy days. A tour includes the gardens, ponds, blacksmith shop, corral, and Winsor Castle (a fortified ranch house). All of these were constructed by Mormons. The fort was built to protect the valuable water supply, the grazing land, and members of the Mormon church.

By 1880, Pipe Spring had declined in importance, but it continued to be used by the church. In 1923, Pipe Spring was declared a national monument by President Warren G. Harding. It remains as "a memorial of western pioneer life."

84

Guided tours of the Pipe Spring fort and grounds are conducted on a regular basis. There's also a do-it-yourself tour. Inquire at the **Visitor Center** for schedules and information.

On your tour, you'll see blacksmith tools, a cheese room where 80 pounds of cheese were made every day, and the first telegraph office in the Arizona Territory (1873).

The **Living History Program** (when volunteers dress in old-style Western costume) is one of Pipe Spring's highlights. You might see butter being churned, cloth being woven, and cattle branding in-season. Guided tours are conducted by uniformed National Park Service personnel.

Take Time...
On your visit to Pipe Spring National Monument, take time to learn about the "real" daily life of a cowboy. Ask questions.

HUBBELL TRADING POST NATIONAL HISTORIC SITE, ARIZONA

In the early 1900s, trading posts were a bridge between two worlds, Indian and Anglo. A visit to Hubbell Trading Post National Historic Site is a chance to learn about a culture different from your own. Hubbell is located on Navajo tribal land, and it's one of the oldest continuously operated trading posts on the reservation. Today, business continues in much the same way it did one hundred years ago. Shelves are stocked with canned goods, and the ceiling is hung with tools, tack, baskets, and buckets. The Hubbell rug room is filled with colorful Navajo rugs and blankets. Silver necklaces, bracelets, and earrings are on display, also. Years ago, Navajo brought weavings, jewelry, wool, and lambs to exchange for trade tokens, instead of official money. They used the tokens to purchase items like canned tomatoes, sardines, Pepto Bismol, evaporated milk, coffee, flour, and calico.

When you visit Hubbell Trading Post, start at the **Visitors Center**, which also has weavings in process and on display. You may be lucky and see a weaver at work.

Ask the ranger about tours around Hubbell Trading Post. He or she might point out where trader John Lorenzo Hubbell's children played. If no tours are available, you can guide yourself with a small map. You will probably come across some noisy chickens on the tour.

Before you leave the Visitors Center, look at the old groceries in the display cases. These are some of the products that were favorites in the old days. At first, Navajo bought only items that had pictures of the product on the outside of the can. Think about it—how would you know what was inside a can if you'd never seen it before? By the label, of course.

Take Time . . .
On your visit to Hubbell Trading Post, take time to think about how things are constantly changing in the world and how you can best adjust to those changes.

SANTA FE TRAIL NATIONAL HISTORIC TRAIL

The Santa Fe Trail served as a major wagon "highway" for almost 60 years (1821-1880). It was an international link between the American East and the untamed Spanish Southwest.

Traders paved the way, followed by homesteaders and fortune hunters. An early trader named William Becknell gets credit as the first to haul his wares along the trail. Mexico had just taken control of the Southwest territory away from Spain. Mexico opened borders and encouraged trade. It took two or three months for loaded wagons to travel from Independence, Missouri, to Santa Fe, New Mexico.

In the early years, fabric, soap, buttons, glass, and tools were popular items on the trip out west. Returning wagons carried furs, mules, silver, and gold from Mexico. Military supplies were also hauled along the trail.

Today, you can still see 150-year-old wagon ruts along the trail. In Colorado and New Mexico, there are plenty of historic stops.

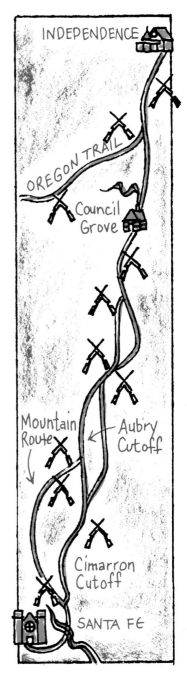

9. The Dare of the Desert

Home hot home! *The desert is only a hostile environment for plants and animals that belong somewhere else. Coyotes, cactus, and lizards are a few of the organisms living happily at home in the desert.*

If you want to find a desert, the American Southwest is a good place to look. You'll discover four separate deserts: the **Chihuahuan**, the **Sonoran**, the **Mohave**, and the **Great Basin**. All have one thing in common—thirst!

How did things get so dry? Blame this lack of water on high mountains and strong westerly winds. Pacific storms "dry out" by the time they blow over the steep coastal mountain ranges. When they reach the desert, total rain and snowfall accumulations aren't much to write home about.

A Matter of Degrees

Sure, deserts are dry, but they aren't always hot, just extreme. Scorching midday temperatures can turn suddenly very chilly as the sun sets. When it finally does rain in the desert, it's probably more like a flood. And desert winds can be nature's sandblasters. Often there's not much shade, and the soil is sparse. Desert predators are hungry and always on the prowl for something (almost anything) good to eat. Very hungry coyotes have been known to eat tennis shoes.

Plants and animals (and people) who make the

desert their home must be adaptable to these extremes or they can't survive for long. Over centuries, even decades, different species continue to evolve and adapt to meet the needs of desert life.

A Desert Survival Kit

A desert tortoise will store one cup of water in its bladder for later thirst quenching. Sidewinder rattlesnakes, coyotes, and owls usually hunt at night when things are cool. Bannertail kangaroo rats digest dry seeds to "create" their own water. Yucca plants adjust their growing rates to stay above blowing sand dunes. The ocotillo plant blossoms only during rainy periods. When it's dry, the ocotillo sheds blossoms and leaves and sits back to wait out the drought. Each of these plants and animals seemingly has its very own survival kit for life in the desert.

What about Me?

We human beings are a very hardy species. See how we've populated (and overpopulated) the world. We adapt to many things, but deserts are not our favorite places. Humans need to drink lots of water. To cool our bodies, we perspire. Our cooling system works, but it's not very efficient when it comes to water conservation. We must frequently replace the water we lose. We can't survive in the desert without a support system that we carry with us—a big canteen. When you visit White Sands National Monument, imagine how you would survive in the dunes for one week. At Scotty's Castle, Death Valley, see how much effort went into cooling off. Over thousands of years, how could human beings change and adapt to drier climates?

Made for each other! The yucca plant and the pronuba moth—theirs is a story of complete and vital co-dependence. Only the yucca can host pronuba youngsters. The pronuba alone can pollinate the yucca blossoms. The blossoms make fine food for the pronuba larvae. All in all, it's a tidy arrangement.

Lions (also called panthers) live in Big Bend National Park. Lions want to be left alone to do their thing, and they want to leave you alone, too. But sometimes meetings occur. What should you do if you encounter a lion? Don't run! Make yourself as big as possible. Stay close to your companions. Wave your hands and shout. Throw stones if the lion is aggressive. Report all sightings to park rangers immediately.

Water, Water Everywhere...

When you spend time in any desert area, take time to really think about water. It's all around you even if you can't see it. Under your feet and below the surface of the earth is groundwater. Some of that water dates back to the time of the last great Ice Age. Oceans, rivers, ponds, and lakes are always evaporating into air. When enough moisture accumulates, the water returns to the earth as rain or snow. Eventually, these same water molecules join rivers and lakes again or seep through underground cracks and faults until they bubble up in natural springs to quench the thirst of living things. Everyone knows that water means life and no water means...

When you think about water in the desert, you understand why we must conserve this refreshing resource.

BIG BEND NATIONAL PARK, TEXAS

It's big! Hike it. Horseback-ride it. River-run it. Bird- and flower-watch it. Fish it. In Big Bend National Park, experience the Chisos Mountains where mountain lions and peregrine falcons roam, river raft white-water rapids, rowboat to Mexico, and explore the Chihuahuan Desert. If you haven't guessed by now, Big Bend is named after a U-turn, or big bend, in the Rio Grande, which borders the park for more than 107 miles.

Park visitor centers, ranger stations, and campgrounds are located at **Rio Grande Village**, **Castolon**, **Persimmon Gap**, **Panther Junction**, and **The Basin** and are also scattered around the park.

Moving Feet

On the **Rio Grande Village Nature Trail**, wander through marshlands and desert, and check out the Rio Grande and Mexico just across the water. Keep your eyes open for beaver activity and ancient fossils. A pair of binoculars makes it easier to bird-watch.

Hot Springs Historic Walk begins at Hot Springs Road. Head for the river where an old bathhouse foundation is a ghostly reminder of Big Bend's pioneers. If the Rio Grande isn't washing out the hot springs, take a relaxing soak. Caution: Do not swim in the Rio Grande. Currents are very strong and very dangerous.

Boquillas Canyon Trail (at Boquillas Canyon) cruises over fossil limestone rock that is 100 million years old! When you reach the river, near the entrance to the canyon, the hefty **sand slide** is perfect for sandy sledding, skidding, and slippery sliding. Go to it! (But use caution! Rocks may be just below the sandy surface.)

Lost Mine Trail is a climb into the **High Chisos Mountains**. Start at **Panther Pass** and keep trekking until you reach an elevation of 6,850 feet. Animals are plentiful, and the views are awesome.

Another good trail for wild creatures watching is 2.2-mile **Burro Spring Trail**. When you reach the spring overlook, sit, look, and listen quietly. If you have patience you may see mule deer, javelina, and wily coyotes. Dusk is a busy time for nature's watering holes. Keep your eyes peeled for animal tracks and droppings.

Window View Trail is short (.10 mile) and easy. Explore the Chisos Basin and watch for del Carmen white-tailed deer. Another way to visit the

The campground at the Basin is #1. Even if the sign on the road says "Campground Full," check it out anyway. There might be an empty space for you.

Que pasa! Skip a rock across the river to Mexico. It's only a stone's throw away. At Boquillas Canyon Overlook, catch a rowboat shuttle to the other side, and burro ride to the Mexican village of Boquillas. It's easy and you don't need your shots or a passport!

V-shaped "window" is a guided trail ride on Chisos Remuda horses.

Overnight or one-day **river raft trips** are great ways to get to know the Rio Grande. Keep your eyes open for river turtles. Ask a ranger for information on off-park river guides.

DEATH VALLEY NATIONAL MONUMENT, CALIFORNIA

How can a place called Death Valley be filled with so much life and so many wonderful things for you to see and do? Are you in the mood to follow animal tracks over huge golden sand dunes? Or how about a 500-foot descent into Ubehebe Crater. Putter around the Devil's Golf Course with all its devilish salt formations. Or explore Scotty's Castle—a millionaire's desert oasis and the symbol of a great friendship. Death Valley National Monument is a big place with endless adventures that await you.

On your way through Death Valley, stop off at the Devil's Golf Course after you enjoy Dante's

Panamint Shoshone Indians have lived in the Death Valley area for many centuries. They helped build Scotty's Castle.

92

View and then drive past the Funeral Mountains, but don't look for Deadman's Pass! There are lots of stories about pioneers, Forty-niners, and explorers who almost died here and christened the valley after their narrow escape. Is that where all these gruesome names came from? No one knows for sure.

Death Valley can be a deadly place only if you forget you're a visitor to some of the lowest, hottest, and driest land on the entire continent. Native plant and animal species have adapted to this extreme environment; you haven't. Always explore with a grown-up. Always tell a friend or ranger where you're going. Always carry and *drink* plenty of water, and wear a hat and sunscreen. Use your common sense!

Furnace Creek Visitor Center is a one-stop oasis if you thirst for knowledge or water. Besides a Death Valley film, slide show, museum exhibits, books, and a schedule of special ranger programs, there are real live rangers who will answer your questions.

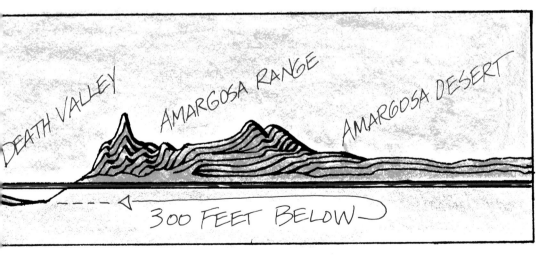

DEATH VALLEY   AMARGOSA RANGE   AMARGOSA DESERT
300 FEET BELOW

Early prospectors dug a well and marked it with a stovepipe so it wouldn't keep getting lost in the shifting sands . . . Stove Pipe Wells!

Furnace Creek also includes a campground, museums, cabins, a post office, restaurants, a grocery store, trail rides, carriage rides, a date palm orchard, and a swimming pool!

Stove Pipe Wells (about 25 miles northwest of Furnace Creek) is the other stop for supplies, snacks, a shower, drinking water, or a dip in the pool.

See? Sí!

Ready for an awesome, mind-boggling view? Tie your shoelaces, because **Zabriskie Point** and **Dante's View** will knock your socks off. Imagine trying to find your way through the orange-pink maze below Zabriskie Point. See the salty flats (almost like a giant skating rink) way down below you and Dante's View. No wonder early travelers dreaded passing through the valley by wooden wagon. How would you find your way over those mountains to the California coast?

Stop!

This valley even has a castle. **Scotty's Castle** is named after Walter E. Scott, a stuntman in the Buffalo Bill Wild West Show, a dreamer, and a tall-tall storyteller.

Scotty convinced several rich folks from the East to "grubstake" his mine in Death Valley. Actually, Scotty only had two souvenir gold nuggets he borrowed from his wife. Albert Johnson, a millionaire from Chicago, decided to invest in Scotty's mine. By the time he discovered it was really "fool's gold," he and Scotty were great friends.

Johnson spent $1½ million to build Scotty's Castle where he and his wife Bessie could vaca-

94

SCOTTY'S CASTLE

tion. Scotty came to visit often. He's buried on Windy Point with his loyal dog, Windy. Take the short hike up. His gravestone reads:

> I got four things to say. Don't say anything that would hurt anybody. Don't give advice—nobody will take it anyway. Don't complain. Don't explain.
>
> Death Valley Scotty
> 1872-1954

Tours of the castle are great fun, and popular. Arrive early in the morning to sign up.

Each room is filled with treasures that rangers will ask you not to touch. Don't feel bad. When park rangers clean the castle, they wear special booties and gloves so they don't damage anything. Come early and ask your ranger to tell you about Scotty's bullet-splitter. The great organ in the annex music room has 1,121 organ pipes that range in size from 16 feet to the size of a soda

There are petroglyphs on rocks near Scotty's Castle. Ask a ranger to show you where to look. Long before Johnson built his castle, early people were living in the area. Natural springs make this a wonderful desert oasis.

The sand dunes are perfect for spotting animal tracks. Kangaroo rats and pack rats, sidewinder rattlesnakes, jackrabbits, and kit foxes all come out in the cool of the night. Speaking of tracks. . .you always know which way the wind went by the dune tracks it left behind.

straw. Listen for various instrument sounds the organ reproduces. What famous song does the organ play? See how many different animals you can find in the house. What's missing from the kitchen? What's so strange about the curtains in the living room?

Ubehebe Crater (near Scotty's Castle) is the perfect volcano vent where you can let off steam. That's what the earth did about 2,000 years ago when red-hot lava rose from below the surface of the earth and encountered groundwater. The super-heat of that meeting caused steam energy many times more powerful than an underground nuclear blast. This resulted in a giant explosion that blasted away layers of rock to form the 500-foot-deep crater.

If you take the 20-minute hike into the crater, don't forget you have to walk back up. Another trail follows the crater rim and a third leads you to **Little Hebe Crater**.

The **Devil's Golf Course** is not the spot for peewee golf, but it's perfect for putting around. The 3- to 5-foot-thick salt crust might look like a giant lemon meringue pie or a space landscape. Salt here is just like the stuff on your kitchen table. If you could reach three miles into the earth beneath your feet, you'd find salt, mud, and sand. This is part of the "salt pan" where groundwater can only travel up. When it evaporates, salt is left behind to be whipped into fantastical shapes by lots of wind and occasional rains.

Where's the sea? Hike into the **sand dunes** and you can imagine ocean waves just over the next dune. These dunes really were mountains at one time. Wind constantly sandblasts bits of rock and gravel from the mountain ranges surround-

ing the dunes. Why don't the dunes just blow away? If the wind always blew one way, they would. But it changes directions according to the season, so the dunes really blow in place. From the shape of the dune ridges, you can tell which way the wind is blowing right now.

Salt Creek is another place that might remind you of oceans. It smells just like a salty seashore. Follow the boardwalk (it's lots of fun and wheelchairs and strollers can cruise here, too) along the creek and look for "pickled" pickleweed and the tiny, darting **Salt Creek pupfish**. This is the only place on earth where Salt Creek pupfish live!

Hike out and talk to the **charcoal kilns**. These ten giant beehives date back to the 1870s. Area trees were burned for charcoal. The charcoal was sent to a smelter and used to refine silver. Step inside. Say something, and let the kilns talk back. It's a weird and eerie echo. Now sniff. Even though the last fires flamed 100 years ago, you smell creosote, a by-product of burning wood.

A trip to **Badwater** is a chance to think about the Badwater snails who live here. Don't walk too close to the edge of the water or you will tread on snail habitat.

A drive to **Artist's Palette** is a journey of color-by-minerals. The reds, pinks, and yellows you see are courtesy of iron salts. Thank decomposing mica for the greens. And manganese brings you the purples. Another bonus: the one-way road twists and dips like a roller coaster.

At the **Borax Museum** (in Furnace Creek), see if you can find an entire mule barn, a giant ox shoeing device, and three stagecoaches. That shouldn't be too hard.

Amazing desert fish!
Death Valley Desert has its very own fish. Some species of desert pupfish can live in water with temperatures higher than 111 degrees and up to 5 times saltier than seawater. Devils Hole pupfish are a unique and endangered species of desert pupfish. Because they are so adaptable to their environment, pupfish are being studied by scientists.

In the 1880s, Chinese workers labored under a blazing sun to construct the 20-mule team road through Death Valley. When you visit Death Valley, imagine working in 120 degree heat!

Borax comes from borates. It's used to make detergents, fertilizers, cosmetics, and fiberglass. In 1881, borax was discovered on the Death Valley salt pan. **Harmony Borax Works** was the site of one refinery. The famous 20-mule teams pulled heavily loaded wagons across the harsh desert. Twenty-mule teams really consisted of 18 mules and 2 horses. The horses were harnessed next to the wagon because of their great strength. The lead mules were 120 feet ahead of the driver. Drivers used 9-foot whips, well-aimed pebbles, and verbal commands to direct the mules. Harnessed in front of the horses, 6 mules (called "pointers") were specially trained to jump over an 80-foot chain that was part of the wagons. A muleskinner (driver) was paid about $4 per day. Special wagons were constructed to haul 12 tons of borax (a full load was more than 60,000 pounds). Twenty-mule teams traveled about 17 miles per day in temperatures as high as 120 degrees.

Take Time...
On your visit to Death Valley National Monument, take time to think about desert ecology and the amazing adaptability of living things.

JOSHUA TREE NATIONAL MONUMENT, CALIFORNIA

If you see them at night, they might look like creatures from another planet, weird sculptures, or marching ghosts. One way or another, the Joshua trees at Joshua Tree National Monument are really incredible.

This monument is shared by two deserts, the arid Colorado Desert and the slightly wetter Mohave Desert where the Joshua trees grow. Add in five palm tree oases and an amazing diversity of wildlife—and that's just the beginning!

Stop at the **Oasis Visitor Center** for park info, exhibits, and schedules of special park programs. This **Oasis of Mara** has been home to Indians, prospectors, and homesteaders.

Nearby, **Fortynine Palms Oasis** has a different clientele—local flora and fauna. The oasis is only a 2.5-kilometer (1.5-mile) hike away. Carry a full canteen, and wear your hat and sunscreen.

At **Hidden Valley trail** (near the Hidden Valley Campground), you'll follow the tracks of an infamous cattle rustler who hid out in this here territory, pardner.

Lost Horse Mine (2.5 kilometers away) is a ghostly reminder of the prospectors and miners who had golden dreams and a pretty parched reality. Always steer clear of abandoned mine shafts for your own safety.

Cholla Cactus Garden is filled with Bigelow cactus, and an easy nature trail gets you acquainted with local plant and animal life.

Grab your binoculars and head for **Cottonwood Spring**, where the birds are. (There's a small visitor center just a mile away.)

The **transition zone** winds throughout the park. This is where the two deserts meet and a unique ecosystem—plants, animals, insects, and other living creatures depending on each other and the earth for survival—has evolved.

Take Time . . .
While you're visiting Joshua Tree National Monument, take time to think about the plants and animals you depend on for food, clothing, shelter, medicine, and many other things. What do you give back in return?

Making a Dune

Gypsum *is a mineral found in the mountains around White Sands. Rain washes it to the basin floor. When the rainwater evaporates, the gypsum crystallizes and becomes brown flaky* **selenite**. *Fierce winds whip the selenite crystals into a collision course until they're blasted into fine white sand particles. Gypsum!*

WHITE SANDS NATIONAL MONUMENT, NEW MEXICO

It's the world's biggest gypsum sand dunes—300 square miles of perpetual motion. It's White Sands National Monument. Ancient Indians, soldiers, pioneers, ranchers, and atomic scientists have all left their footprints on the dunes. These days you'll see a variety of shoe treads (including Nike and Adidas) as you walk.

The **visitor center** has exhibits, posters, books, and rangers, too. Enter the park and cruise the 25-kilometer (16-mile) **Heart of the Dunes** loop to brush up on dunefield ecology and geology.

Along the way, you may spot a strange-looking creature called an **oryx**, or African antelope. These exotic animals really belong in the Kalahari Desert. What are they doing here? Probably creating problems for native plant and animal species. Originally introduced into surrounding areas by the New Mexico Game and Fish Department, the oryx have trespassed onto national parklands. They're surviving so well in the park, they're pushing out native animals.

Stop! The one-mile **self-guided nature trail** into the dunes is fun, fascinating, and easy. Keep an eye out for lizard, pocket mouse, beetle, or roadrunner tracks in the sand. There's skunk-brush sumac to sniff and fossilized roots to discover. Feel the sand with your fingers. This is 97% pure gypsum and it feels like what—cornmeal, cake flour, snow on Jupiter?

A ranger-guided tour to **Lake Lucero** usually happens the last weekend of every month. These take about four hours and they're fascinating. You'll examine the strange and beautiful selenite crystals along the shores of the lake, and the ranger will answer your questions.

Don't forget, the dunefield ecosystem is very delicate. Tread lightly and be considerate of the creatures and plants who live here.

Take Time...
On your visit to White Sands National Monument, take time to learn about a desert creature and how it adapts to its environment.

*White Sands National Monument has an unusual next door neighbor, **White Sands Missile Range**. Area roads and the park itself close down when missile testing is in progress. A portion of the park is a "joint use" area. It is shared by the park and the military.*

10. Back to the Future

Share your travel discoveries! Send me your tips, recommendations, and gripes, and help keep this book up-to-the-minute: Sarah Lovett, P.O. Box 613, Santa Fe, NM 87504.

The year is 2095. You're twelve years old and you live in a big city like almost every human on Planet Earth. But you've heard stories and myths about the old days when there were awesome forests, crystal clear lakes, and wild elk, wolves, and bears. Where can you go to see wilderness?

No one can take the future for granted. It's up to us to ensure that national parks exist in 100 years so that kids in 2095 can share what we have today.

If it weren't for conservationists who lived 100 years ago, we would not have some of the beautiful parks that you will visit this year. Efforts to conserve, protect, and add more wilderness land to the National Park System must continue forever. A label, even "national park," can't guarantee protection. But we can.

National Parks Need Your Help!
National Parks are faced with many problems today: too many people, not enough water, pollution, and endangered species are just a few. But there are lots of ways we can help national parks.

Learn how to enjoy nature the low-impact way. Become a specialist on ecology, geology,

What if someone suddenly gave you 50,000 acres of wilderness to take care of so that kids living in the year 2095 could experience nature? What would you need to know to do the job right?

In 1964, Congress passed the Wilderness Act. That means land can be set aside and protected from development. No roads, no motor vehicles, no permanent human traces! Once it's wilderness, it's up to us to keep it that way.

archaeology, and/or natural history. Get to know park rangers. Adopt a park and make its concerns your business. Ask questions. And then speak out and teach others. Nothing can replace the wildness and wonder of wilderness!

Appendix

Arches National Park
P.O. Box 907
Moab, UT 84532
801-259-8161

Bandelier National Monument
Los Alamos, NM 87544
505-672-3861

Big Bend National Park
Big Bend National Park, TX 79834
915-477-2251

Bryce Canyon National Park
Bryce Canyon, UT 84717
801-834-5322

Canyon de Chelly National Monument
P.O. Box 588
Chinle, AZ 86503
602-674-5436

Canyonlands National Park
125 West 200 South
Moab, UT 84532
801-259-7164

Capitol Reef National Park
Torrey, UT 84775
801-425-3791

Capulin National Monument
Capulin, NM 88414
505-278-2201

Carlsbad Caverns National Park
3225 National Parks Highway
Carlsbad, NM 88220
505-785-2232

Chaco Canyon National Historical Park
Star Route 4, Box 6500
Bloomfield, NM 87413
505-988-6727

Death Valley National Monument
Death Valley, CA 92328
619-786-2331

Dinosaur National Monument
P.O. Box 210
Dinosaur, CO 81610
303-374-2216

El Morro National Monument
Rahmah, NM 87321
505-783-4226

Fort Davis National Historic Site
P.O. Box 1456
Fort Davis, TX 79734
915-426-3337

Fort Union National Monument
Watrous, NM 87753
505-425-8025

Grand Canyon National Park
P.O. Box 129
Grand Canyon, AZ 86023
602-638-7770

Great Basin National Park
Baker, NV 89311
702-234-7331

Hubbell Trading Post National Historic Site
P.O. Box 150
Ganado, AZ 86505
602-755-3254

Joshua Tree National Monument
74485 National Monument Drive
Twentynine Palms, CA 92277
619-367-7511

Mesa Verde National Park
Mesa Verde National Park, CO 81330
303-529-4461

Petrified Forest National Park
Petrified Forest National Park, AZ 86028
602-524-6228

Pipe Spring National Monument
Moccasin, AZ 86022
602-643-7105

San Antonio Missions National Historic Park
2202 Roosevelt Avenue
San Antonio, TX 78210
512-229-5701

Sunset Crater National Monument
Route 3, Box 149
Flagstaff, AZ 86004
602-527-7042

Timpanogos Cave National Monument
R.R. 3, Box 200
American Fork, UT 84003
801-756-5238

White Sands National Monument
P.O. Box 458
Alamogordo, NM 88310
505-479-6124

Zion National Park
Springdale, UT 84767-1099
801-772-3256

Kidding Around with John Muir Publications

We are making the world more accessible for young travelers. In your hand you have one of several John Muir Publications guides written and designed especially for kids. We will be *Kidding Around* other cities also. Send us your thoughts, corrections, and suggestions. We also publish other books about travel and other subjects. Let us know if you would like one of our catalogs.

TITLES NOW AVAILABLE IN THE SERIES

Kidding Around Atlanta
Kidding Around Boston
Kidding Around Chicago
Kidding Around the Hawaiian Islands
Kidding Around London
Kidding Around Los Angeles
**Kidding Around the National Parks
    of the Southwest**
Kidding Around New York City
Kidding Around Philadelphia
Kidding Around San Francisco
Kidding Around Washington, D.C.

John Muir Publications
P.O. Box 613
Santa Fe, New Mexico 87504
(505) 982-4078